T0341948

Revolutionizing
Trauma Treatment

Revolutionizing Trauma Treatment

Stabilization, Safety, & Nervous System Balance

BABETTE ROTHSCHILD

W. W. NORTON & COMPANY
Independent Publishers Since 1923

The author welcomes correspondence from readers. She may be reached at:
Babette Rothschild
P.O. Box 241778, Los Angeles, California 90024
Telephone: 310 281 9646
E-mail: babette@sttwork.com
Website: www.trauma.cc

For information about permission to reproduce selections from this book, write to Permissions, W. W. Norton & Company, Inc., 500 Fifth Avenue, New York, NY 10110

For information about special discounts for bulk purchases, please contact W. W. Norton Special Sales at specialsales@wwnorton.com or 800-233-4830

Manufacturing by LSC Harrisonburg
Production manager: Katelyn MacKenzie

Library of Congress Cataloging-in-Publication Data
Names: Rothschild, Babette, author.
Title: Revolutionizing trauma treatment : stabilization, safety, & nervous system balance / Babette Rothschild.
Description: New York, N.Y. : W.W. Norton & Company, [2021] |
"A Norton professional book." | Includes bibliographical references and index.
Identifiers: LCCN 2020056670 | ISBN 9781324016724 (paperback) |
ISBN 9781324016731 (epub)
Subjects: LCSH: Post-traumatic stress disorder—Treatment. |
Psychic trauma—Treatment. | Mind and body therapies.
Classification: LCC RC489.M53 R682 2021 | DDC 616.85/2106—dc23
LC record available at https://lccn.loc.gov/2020056670

W. W. Norton & Company, Inc., 500 Fifth Avenue, New York, N.Y. 10110
www.wwnorton.com

W. W. Norton & Company Ltd., 15 Carlisle Street, London W1D 3BS

1 0 9 8 7 6 5 4 3

to, for, and from

Joe

with Love and Gratitude

I Am Free

Clare Jones

When the ghosts of my past whisper to me
I say, "I am free"
I open my eyes and I see
Pinks, blues, reds and orange
Yellow, purple, turquoise is my favourite
A world of rich tapestry

When the ghosts of my past shout loudly at me
I say "NO" firmly
I open my ears and I hear
Birds singing, engines purring, people talking, laughing
I look, I see
The ghosts are not here with me
Leaves falling, children playing, couple arguing, man smoking

When the ghosts feel too close to my skin
I feel
The ground beneath my feet
The breeze touching my face
The warmth of the sun
The fabric inside my pocket, against my hand
A touching embrace

The ghosts cannot compete
With the power of nature
I see
I hear
I feel
I taste
Delicious distractions
Like honey, smooth and sweet
Bitter chocolate, juicy orange, sugary treat

The ghosts are far away now
I am safe
I see my friends, my colleagues, my family
I am here, now
I am free

I know
The ghosts are ghosts
They are not here now
They cannot hurt me
I am free

Contents

Introduction to the Paperback Edition

I am tremendously excited for *Revolutionizing Trauma Treatment* (previously published in hardback as *The Body Remembers, Volume 2*), to now be issued in this paperback edition. Paperback books are always more affordable and therefore available to a broader readership. I believe in what I write and love that now more of you will be able to be exposed to my point of view. I hope you find it of use!

Truth be told, of all the books I've written, this one holds a special place in my heart. There is more of me professionally and personally, and more of my heart and soul in this volume. I guess that is because I am older and more professionally established, and perhaps because this is the sixth book I have written. As I was drafting it, I felt more free to be myself and say, candidly, what I believe to be important despite the (nearly guaranteed) risk of disagreement and criticism. For example, that is why I felt I could dare to title this paperback edition, *Revolutionizing Trauma Treatment*. I admit that it is sort of arrogant to make such a claim, but I sincerely hope that is the realization of this book: to revolutionize the way much of trauma treatment is viewed and trauma therapy is conducted.

Some of you might wonder what it is that I believe is revolutionizing in this book and why I believe the field of trauma treatment could be bettered through, what I believe to be, my revolutionary point of view. In the preface and the first chapter, I make my case for this viewpoint, and then throughout the book I continue to support my perspective. Briefly, though, let me just say here: In general practice, there is still way too much emphasis on routinely applying interpretations and conclusions drawn from the *evidence base* without consideration of potential limitations or individual differences. In addition, it is still a common practice to forge ahead with processing trauma memories often at the cost of adequate attention to the traumatized individual's needs, symptoms, preferences, abilities, current life situation, and so on. Because of that, there are all too many people in need who fall through the cracks! The first case, on the first page of the first chapter, is just one very sad example. The revolutionizing remedies that I propose throughout these pages demonstrate the importance of making multiple options for recovering from trauma known *and* available to *both* therapists and clients, and in recognition and respect for those who do not want, or are not safely able, to process memories.

As previously noted, the title for this paperback edition has been changed to *Revolutionizing Trauma Treatment*, which was the original subtitle of the hardback version. Of course, changing the title raises the question of why a different title and the addition of the new subtitle, *Stabilization, Safety, and Nervous System Balance*? The answer is two-fold.

The title change reflects what those who have read the hardback version have consistently told me they most relate to: What I am proposing here is, indeed, a *revolution* in trauma treatment. Bringing the subtitle, *Revolutionizing Trauma Treatment*, forward to be the title highlights the true intention of the book and will hopefully make it more visible and easier to find. So, to be clear, *this* book, *Revolutionizing Trauma Treatment*, is *not* a revision of *The Body Remembers* (2000), but a continuation of the discussion and ideas that were begun there. *Revolutionizing Trauma Treatment* reflects both the evolution of my own experience and thinking as well as, for better and for worse, the growth and changes in the fields of trauma studies and trauma treatment over the 20 years since *The Body Remembers* was first published.

The subtitle change, *Stabilization, Safety, and Nervous System Balance*, is in part a response to the overwhelmingly enthusiastic reception of my significant attention to the nervous system as a whole, including the color fold-out of the autonomic nervous system (ANS) table (following page 66). The ANS table has stimulated immense interest and been utilized well beyond readers of the book, defying *all* expectations. Instructors, clinics, practice groups, and clients themselves have all adopted the ANS table, often in the form of the separately available laminated card version (* see footnote, below), as their most useful tool for monitoring and modulating ANS arousal. I always hoped it would be a useful contribution so I am *very* happy to see my hope realized! For those of you who have chosen this paperback volume seeking more information on the ANS table, look to Chapter 2 for a lengthy discussion on its development and usage. Throughout the book, there are also numerous examples of applying the information interpreted from the ANS table in practice with clients, as well as for practitioner self-care to aid in preventing vicarious trauma and compassion fatigue.

Feedback on my emphasis of stabilization and safety as a critical foundation for trauma recovery, including applications of the *sensory nervous system* into practice, has also been extremely positive. While nearly every book, class, and training for prospective and experienced trauma therapists includes theory and applications of the ANS, few pay adequate attention to the importance of stabilization and safety or give the sensory nervous system its due. There is tremendous value to be gained from understanding how the sensory system works. Such knowledge has the potential to make stabilization *much* easier, quicker, and more reliable, while also making any trauma therapy safer. In addition, simple applications from sensory nervous system theory will make mindful practices (including meditation, mindfulness based stress reduction, and yoga) more widely accessible to a greater number of traumatized individuals.

I wish to extend many thanks to my editor, Deborah Malmud, and the entire editorial board at W. W. Norton & Co. for believing in and supporting this paperback reissue of *Revolutionizing Trauma Treatment: Stabilization, Safety, and Nervous System Balance*. Here's hoping that many more practitioners and their clients benefit!

---

*The laminated version of the ANS table is available from wwnorton.com and online booksellers including amazon.com and amazon.co.uk. It has numerous advantages including the possibility to write on it with a whiteboard dry erase marker (do *not* use permanent ones!), so you can track your or your clients' arousal level. Then you can erase it and use it for the next. Many clients also like to have their own for the same purpose.

Introduction

This book, *Revolutionizing Trauma Treatment* (previously published as *The Body Remembers*, Volume 2) continues the discussion I began in my first book, *The Body Remembers: The Psychophysiology of Trauma and Trauma Treatment* (Rothschild, 2000). As soon as that book went to press, I knew there was more that I wanted to contribute to the field of traumatic stress to continue to improve and expand treatment options for those impacted by trauma. The four books I've published since have broadened the discussion, but I have always wanted to return to expanding on the foundations of the first. In this second volume I will do just that. That means that this is *not* a revision of *The Body Remembers*, but a stand-alone book in its own right that is linked to it. (You can make use of this book without having read the first volume.)

In the years since my first book was published, I have continued in my capacity as psychotherapist, body psychotherapist, and trauma therapist while practicing, teaching, lecturing, supervising, and consulting around the world. My professional programs have been attended by tens of thousands from all corners of the helping professions, representing every educational level, theoretical background, and available method of trauma therapy. I consistently receive feedback (and book sales confirm) that the theory, principles, and tools offered in that first volume continue to be relevant and accessible to practitioners (and also self-help readers) of all sorts.

Through my own work with clients as well as listening to the questions, failures, concerns, challenges, and successes of those attending my programs, I have, I believe, gained further insight into the conundrum of post-traumatic stress disorder (PTSD) as well as a greater understanding of how to ease the suffering of the many who are plagued by it—particularly those who are falling through the cracks of mental health systems. On a regular basis I receive e-mails and calls from individuals (and family members representing them) who are suffering because of agencies and practitioners who are rigidly bound by managed care, evidence-based practice, agency and health service guidelines, and the like. I also receive regular cries for help from professionals who are frustrated and concerned when forced to apply methods and limit sessions in ways they know are not right for one or more clients. These system failures are of increasing concern to me and spur much of the energy behind this volume.

This may turn out to be a controversial book. I want to broaden the options available to trauma clients.* To do so, throughout I will be challenging trauma therapists to think about why they do what they do, the decisions they are making—every intervention—and to consider alternatives in relationship to the *individual* they are working with. Moreover, I have always been of the belief that differing points of view are necessary for the growth and development of any field of study, also in the profession of traumatic stress. Where there is only agreement, there is stagnation. So I hope that you will feel challenged rather than put off by topics or ideas in this book that you disagree with, that you will be open to considering different points of view. Please consider those as opportunities to refine your own point of view and develop your own direction. Of course I also hope that there will be plenty of areas that you find of value and use, that add to your understanding and skill set. Really, there should be some of both if this book is to make the significant contribution to your and other readers' professional development that I am aiming for.

It is my further hope that this volume will be added to the required reading of university courses and training programs of diverse disciplines

---

* I use abbreviated terminology such as *trauma client* and *trauma therapist* instead of terms that may be more comfortable for some, such as *clients who have experienced trauma* and *therapists who work with clients who have experienced trauma*. Hopefully, by doing so, reading this book will flow more smoothly.

of trauma theory and treatment, encouraging students to consider various (also opposing) points of view and begin to formulate their own opinions. Such considered thinkers will be in a much better position to tailor trauma treatment to their clients on an individual basis rather than adopting one theory base and methodology to uniformly apply to everyone.

As with all of my books, I endeavor to make each chapter accessible to, and relevant for, practitioners working with every population (gender, age, culture, and so on) and specializing in any method or model.

Disclaimer

There is a similar disclaimer placed in each of my books and that I deliver at the beginning of every lecture and training I present. This has been my custom for more than two decades. I began including this disclaimer as a protest to the many of my own teachers and colleagues who believe they are imparting *truth*. Once I realized that truth, per se, does not exist, at least not in psychotherapy, I decided to make sure that those I taught knew that truth was *not* something I was selling. My disclaimer goes like this.

Every bit of information and each treatment procedure discussed in this book is based on theory and speculation. That is not because there is anything wrong with these contents, but because theory and speculation are all we really have. There is *nothing* in psychology or the area of traumatic stress studies and treatment that is hard fact. Nothing we know for sure. Actually, the same is true for the vast majority of science and medicine. The thing about knowledge is that it changes all the time—that is how it evolves. This means that every book, training program, method, intervention, and so on in psychology and trauma therapy is also based on theory and speculation—no matter how assured the author, teacher, or creator sounds. Again, nothing wrong here; this is just how knowledge develops.

In this same vein, Antonio Damasio (1994), a highly respected neuroscientist, reminds us that science consists of approximations that we use until better ones come along. In no way is this a failure of science or of the field of traumatic stress. It is a very normal process of knowledge and professional development. Where it can be a problem is when approximations are taken to be certainty. More on this below.

Understanding that facts and sure things do not exist in psychology and psychotherapy is integral to understanding some of the difficulties we face in helping our traumatized clients. One of these is the shortcoming of trying to apply the *evidence base* to all situations. I will expand on this in the preface that follows, but for now, in the spirit of this disclaimer, I will just tell you that there is *no* medication or treatment for PTSD that helps more than 50% of clients. This is not a problem in itself as this is consistent in the field of medicine—treatments and medications work for merely a percentage of patients. (That is why, as you may have noticed, there is such a long list of warnings and disclaimers that accompanies advertising for medications and medical procedures on television, radio, and in print.) However, it does become a problem when treatments adopted into the evidence base become misinterpreted or promoted as beneficial for all. It is important to note that every teacher and author who cites or quotes studies that support his or her point of view is also *not* quoting from or citing those that do *not*. And, for the most part, I have to include myself in this. No one who is trying to sway you to their position is (usually) going to tell you what the opposition has to say. When reading a book or listening to a lecture, just remember that the writer or speaker is expressing *opinions* and that opinions are *not* facts. The reader's or student's task is to formulate his or her own, individual opinion—whether or not that agrees with the teacher or author. Who is to say which one is correct?

I routinely caution my audiences that I will never let a discussion digress into who is right and who is wrong because I do not believe those exist. And I always end by telling them, as I will tell you now: I pride myself on being paid for my opinions, *not* to be right. That means that when a colleague, student, or client disagrees with me, I always consider that their point of view could be the correct one, even as I might believe in and argue strongly for my standpoint.

Basic Definitions

Throughout this book I will be relying on the basic definition of *post-traumatic stress disorder* (PTSD) as agreed upon for the fifth edition of the *Diagnostic and Statistical Manual of Mental Disorders* (*DSM-5*) (American Psychiatric Association, 2013). That is, PTSD can result from "exposure to actual or threatened death, serious injury, or sexual violence" (p. 271) experienced either directly, as a witness, through learning about death or violence happening to someone close, or repeated exposure to spoken or visual details of death or violence (for example, police, lawyers, juries, doctors, therapists, counselors, and so on). A second *DSM-5* diagnostic category, *acute stress disorder* (ASD), is similar to PTSD, but lasts for one month or less. If symptoms do not resolve within that time period, PTSD becomes the diagnosis. It is important to note that both PTSD and ASD are *event dependent*. That is, without an identifiable traumatic event, the diagnosis cannot be PTSD or ASD. This point is vital in guiding safe trauma treatment: No matter how suspicious it appears that a traumatic incident may have occurred, if it is not *identifiable*—actually remembered, witnessed, or recorded in some way—treatment must focus on the here-and-now issues and symptoms, *not* on trying to piece together a past that may or may not exist. Otherwise the risk of creating or reinforcing *false memory* (Courtois, 1999) is just too great.

It is also noted in the *DSM-5* that those who are diagnosed with PTSD have an 80% higher chance than those without that diagnosis to have symptoms of one or more additional mental disorders. Of course that increases the challenge of trauma treatment. Readers are cautioned to consider their own professional (and personal) situations in making use of and integrating the points of view on PTSD as expressed in this volume. Any of the trauma situations described herein could be complicated by other mental health conditions. However, it would not be possible to address all of those possibilities. Therefore, these theories, principles, and tools are limited to the specifics involved in trauma treatment. Where additional concurrent disorders are present, practitioners and clients together will need to make their decisions on the priorities of and approach to the therapy.

A Controversial Point of View

Do you have clients who during or between sessions:

- Are decompensating?
- Easily dissociate?
- Continue to have anxiety or panic attacks?
- Suffer repeated flashbacks?
- Lose contact with themselves?
- Lose contact with you?
- And so on.

These are just some of the common challenges faced by therapists and their clients that I am hoping to address with this book. Increasingly over the last 15 years I've had both clients and therapists seeking consultation with me because of adverse experiences with many types and models of trauma therapy. Sometimes I could help them easily. But sometimes the difficulties were more complex. Either way, among these many consultations, several common themes emerged:

- The therapy was prematurely focused on processing trauma memories.
- The direction of the therapy was unclear.
- The therapist's agenda had superseded the client's.
- Whatever the therapeutic focus, it was clearly too much for the client.
- The aim of the therapy was to "relive" traumatic experiences.
- What precipitated the client into therapy had been put aside or forgotten.
- Client stabilization had not been a priority or was not given adequate time.

The specialized field of traumatic stress studies and its practice component, trauma treatment, is now nearly 40 years old. In those years, as a profession, we have had numerous successes, though also way too many failures. It is important to learn from and better our work from both—I am a *big* fan of the value of learning from mistakes (the students in my 12-day trainings can attest to this). And, I believe, there has been a big mistake made in the field of traumatic stress: In general, as a profession, we have made a huge error in how we routinely treat traumatized clients. Based in Freud's *talking cure*, trauma therapy has, traditionally, depended on the telling of the client's trauma story as the basis for the healing. Virtually all models of trauma treatment depend on—to one degree or another—the narration (usually in great detail) of one or more traumatic events. While I, and just about everyone I know, would agree that this does, indeed, help a good many people (particularly at the right time and under the best of circumstances), there is also a growing recognition that significant numbers of patients and clients actually are hurt, even retraumatized, by this practice.

Unfortunately, I cannot find statistics to back up this opinion. In fact, no one is writing about or making research studies on treatment *failures*. Those statistics are hidden in the dropout and noncompliance figures (for example, Imel, Laska, Jakupcak, & Simpson, 2013), lost work time, hospitalizations, and such. Most all of these issues are talked about privately, professional to professional, peer confiding to peer, and as dilemmas raised in supervision and during consultations. It does not appear to be something we as a profession like to advertise. However, I can attest that I receive all too many e-mails and phone requests for help along these lines, and that discussion of this topic consistently brings enthusiastic feedback from therapists in my lectures and trainings. The practitioners in the trenches do know about these limitations but are often dissuaded from or embarrassed to talk about them. In bringing this issue into the open, I am hoping to influence greater attention to these problems among the administrators and others who are creating treatment guidelines and directing therapists in implementing them. Treatment failures are particularly hidden when professionals—for whatever reason—are limited to adhering to a single model for trauma treatment. A good example of such risks was demonstrated by an offhand comment during a seminar I attended. The speaker was discussing the benefits and limitations of a popular, evidence-based, method for treating trauma and PTSD. During the question segment, someone from the audience asserted in a voice filled with irritation, "Well I use [that method] exclusively and I *never* have *any* of those problems!" I thought at the time, and still do, that this comment perfectly summed up the hazards of only having one tool available. I imagine she could not afford to be aware of the limitations of (that method—really, insert *any* single method) because she had no others to offer, nothing else in her toolbox. In such circumstances, if something goes awry in the therapy, the blame must go to the client. How could the method be blamed if it is the only one available?

A Few Words About Control

Loss of control is at the core of PTSD. No one develops the disorder who was in control of the circumstances: able to stop the car or the tsunami, not be in the wrong place at the wrong time, avoid the perpetrator, and so on. Further, people with PTSD have a multitude of highly distressing mind and body symptoms that characterize the disorder and appear beyond their control, including intrusive memories in the form of visual, auditory, or somatic flashbacks that come unbidden and rock their stability. PTSD is, really, all about losing control. Therefore, it makes a lot of sense to prioritize reclaiming and increasing a client's sense of control over his or her body, mind, therapy situation, and life. Judith Herman (1992), one of the early pioneers in the field of trauma treatment, in her seminal book *Trauma and Recovery* wrote, "The first principle of recovery is empowerment of the survivor. She must be the author and arbiter of her own recovery" (p. 133). As well as being common sense, researchers are also looking at the importance of reinstating control. Alim et al. (2008) found that helping individuals to gain a sense of mastery was an important factor in trauma recovery. Whether specifically mentioned or not, every theory, principle, intervention, and guideline in this book is placed here with that in mind: to increase clients' control over their mind, body, and life.

About This Book

Revolutionizing Trauma Treatment (previously published as *The Body Remembers*, Volume 2) follows the same structure as the first volume by organizing the contents into two sections: Theory and Principles, and Practice: Applying Theory and Principles. Also consistent with the first volume, this second volume will feature, and weave throughout, applications of body awareness, body memory, and body resources as valuable adjuncts to trauma treatment. In addition, most chapters will be complemented by descriptive case studies or annotated therapy session transcripts. These will help the ideas to come alive by putting them into practice. Where possible, I have chosen cases and sessions which not only demonstrate the topic of that particular chapter or section, but also pull together multiple concepts highlighted throughout the book. Each case and session will be carefully described and include references to the relevant passages (both previous and forthcoming). In this way, I hope to demonstrate that many principles can be blended and integrated in varying combinations to maximize *individualized* therapy, safety, and effectiveness. Please note that all clients discussed in this book are actually composites of multiple clients and that all identifying information has been altered or deleted. This makes possible a free and in-depth discussion of the pertinent issues and principles without any threat to personal confidentiality. Therefore, therapists and clients might recognize familiar themes but can be confident that no case discussion is specifically about themselves or anyone they might know.

You may be wondering at this point whether or not you need to read *The Body Remembers* to be able to make use of this book. Please be assured that I have been careful to write this book as a fully separate, readable, and applicable book of its own. Many colleagues have generously helped by reading and commenting on various stages of the manuscript (see the acknowledgments), some who have and some who have not read the first volume. With their feedback, and the careful attention of myself and my editor, we have made sure that *no one* needs to read the first volume—or any of my other books—to understand and make use of this book.

Part I, Theory and Principles

The stable foundation formed by a wide variety of theories and principles makes it possible for every therapy to be nuanced and individually tailored to the needs of a specific client. That firm base will also increasingly help you to better ensure benefit from any techniques you choose and make them safer to apply. Likewise, the more diverse and confident you become in your knowledge of theory and principles, the less dependent you will be on techniques developed by others. Your increased understanding will give you a solid position from which to create interventions that will target particular client needs. The theory and principle discussions in this chapter are meant as additions to, *not* replacements for, those you have previously acquired and will gain in the future. My aim is to *expand* your knowledge base and tool kit, *never* to shrink it.

Chapter 1, "Revolutionizing Trauma Treatment," challenges the commonly accepted notion that clients with PTSD must revisit, review, and process their memories in order to recover from their traumas. An expanded range of avenues for healing is explored, increasing total options for all those affected by trauma.

Chapter 2, "Precision ANS Regulation: What to Look For," updates, expands, and integrates understanding of the autonomic nervous system (ANS) across both traditional and more recent theoretical viewpoints. A new, innovative full-color tool to enhance and simplify your ability to monitor and regulate your clients' (and your own) ANS will be introduced.

Chapter 3, "Safety Requires *All* the Senses: Sensory Stabilization," identifies that a major key to stabilizing the dysregulation caused by traumatic stress lies in balancing access to the sensory nervous system—an often neglected area of trauma theory and treatment.

Chapter 4, "Revitalizing a Lost Art: Trauma Treatment Planning," identifies the disappearance of this lost art and promotes rigorous assessment, history taking, and treatment planning as an integral part of every course of trauma therapy.

Part II, Practice: Applying Theory and Principles

The tools and interventions in this section are not meant as step-by-step recipes. The most important aspects of these discussions and demonstrations are the principles that underlie the interventions. I hope you will pay most attention to those so that, where appropriate, you will be able to apply the principles differently than is demonstrated here. In this way you will ensure that you are tailoring your therapy decisions to the needs of individual clients rather than applying the same interventions to everyone.

Chapter 5, "Simple Resources Modulate and Even Heal Trauma," shows that trauma therapy does not need to be traumatizing. Everyone has resources, even the most debilitated. The trick is to identify and cultivate resources that already exist, making them accessible in everyday situations. Accessing resources will temper the intensity of the therapy and the impact of the trauma, and help to improve quality of life.

Chapter 6, "Making the Most of Good Memories," recognizes that not all memories are bad ones. And, in fact, good memories from the past can be valuable adjuncts to mediating the negative effects of traumatic memories. Damasio's theory of *somatic markers* will be applied to the creation of effective antidotes to many trauma symptoms.

Chapter 7, "Pacing, Portioning, and Organizing," features strategies for making the processing of trauma memories easier and safer.

Chapter 8, "Adapting Mindfulness, MBSR, and Yoga for Those With PTSD," recognizes that not all clients are able to make use of mindful practices. Integrating theory from Chapter 3, applications of mindfulness are adjusted to the needs of those with disrupted nervous systems. In addition, there will be a report from a pilot study that adapted mindfulness-based stress reduction specifically to the needs of those with PTSD. Last, mindfulness applications for practitioner self-care will be reviewed.

The appendix, "Trauma Therapist Beware: Avoiding Common Hazards," will help practitioners to identify and avoid some of the most widespread mistakes that I have observed others (and myself!) make repeatedly. I also hope to make the topic of therapeutic errors more comfortable to look for, admit to, and talk about for the benefit of colleagues and clients alike.

Caveat on Applying Techniques and Strategies

There are some exceptions to the tool and principle recommendations throughout this volume. It is important to remember that this book is concerned with the treatment of traumatized individuals and PTSD. The interventions recommended here may or may not work for people with other, multiple, additional, or concurrent diagnoses or complicating factors. Such exceptions include psychosis, bipolar disorder, depression, substance abuse, and traumatic brain injury. Treatment of those and other disorders is beyond the scope of this book. That does not mean you cannot try any of these same strategies with those types of clients. However, though I offer the tools herein with confidence for use with PTSD, I cannot say the same for their application with other types of mental disorders.

Revolutionizing Trauma Treatment

Research Bias and the Evidence Base

This preface dovetails with my belief about opinions as expressed in the disclaimer section in the introduction. Even the best medical advice is based on opinion rather than fact. But human faith in *the authority* is usually difficult to contradict. People generally want to believe that the doctor, therapist, researcher, and so on, *knows*. I often hear from family members or friends of mine, when they're struggling with a challenging medical condition, "I'll just do what my doctor tells me. She knows what to do." The problem here is that all any doctor has available is also her opinion. None of them knows. One of the best examples I have comes from my own personal experience. Some years ago, while I was suffering from a bout of unrelenting irritable bowel syndrome (IBS), I coincidentally had previously scheduled consultations with three different physicians for varying other issues: a gastroenterologist, a cardiologist, and my primary care internist. I took advantage of these appointments, which were meant for other things, to also get a grip on the IBS. My primary care doctor advised me to "eat only rice and chicken for a week." The cardiologist told me, "Stick to clear liquids for several days to give your system a rest." Last, the gastroenterologist directed me, "Eat whatever you want and take Imodium as needed." So I ask you, who knew the truth? Which treatment recommendation was correct and based on facts? The answer in this situation is clear: not one of them really *knew* what would help. They were expressing their opinions, not facts. As a result, I further learned to depend on paying careful attention to the reactions of my own body to guide me in healing the IBS.

This brings me to the *evidence base*. Though often believed to be the bastion of truth, it, too, is composed of opinions. There are *no* facts in the evidence base. Some of you reading the previous sentence may feel relieved to be confirmed in what you already suspected. Others may be confused or disappointed to find out that what you thought was a secure guiding light may not be quite so sure or always illuminating. And a portion of you might firmly disagree with me. Whatever your position, the good news is that there is relevance to be found in research if you know how to interpret it, and how to apply that interpretation.

First of all, I would recommend that you read the little book called *How to Lie With Statistics* by Darrell Huff. Still in print, it was first published in 1954 and continues to be a best-selling, highly accessible, valuable little volume. It was the first book I was required to read for my beginning-level university psychology course. With tongue in cheek, Huff illuminates how statistics of all sorts can be manipulated to support whichever point of view is being promoted. Marketers, drug manufacturers, and, yes, even adherents of various trauma treatment models all participate in shaping how outcomes are expressed in order to promote whatever they are selling. Understanding this does not mean that you need to discount all research, but it will make you a more savvy reader. Here's an example.

Recently, a friend was discussing a new cancer treatment a relative of his was considering. He read from the manufacturer's brochure that the particular medicine was shown to *reduce and eliminate* tumors in 50% of patients. That caught my attention and I asked him to see if there was any specific percentage quoted for the numbers of patients whose tumors were eradicated. My Huff-inspired reasoning was that if the number of patients whose tumors completely disappeared was large, they would not have lumped it together with those who had reduced tumor size. Sure enough, on further reading he found a small note that 41% of patients had reduced tumor size and it was only in 9% that tumors disappeared. Do not misunderstand: This is not actually deception as the correct percentages were available, just hidden so not obvious on first reading. But it is one way in which research outcomes can be maneuvered to bolster a particular point of view. In this case, that means possibly implying a more positive outcome than might be warranted.

Another example comes from therapists at my lectures and trainings. During lecture or discussion of brain science, someone often cites research claiming "trauma shrinks the hippocampus." This is always stated as a fact. Then I ask, how can you be sure that is certain? That may be the case in the mice they study, but does the same thing happen in humans? To know that would require a large number of people to have brain scans *prior* to experiencing trauma and then be scanned again following trauma. Think about the expense and complexities in conducting such a research study: Among other things, the subjects would have to agree to the scans and then to be followed during their lives on the lookout for traumatic events. I doubt many would want to participate.

What About the Evidence Base?

Truth be told, I am not a fan of overreliance on what we call *evidence-based practice*. There are many reasons, including the ones discussed above. The origin of the concept of the evidence base included anecdotal evidence. That is, individual experience and observation were a part of the evidence. But somehow that has gotten deleted from the current concept, which means individual therapist and client experience does not officially count. One may argue that anecdotal evidence is too biased. However, it is important to note that *all* of the evidence base is biased. The evidence base in trauma therapy, psychotherapy, and psychopharmacology is solely dependent on outcome research. While all research is inherently biased (Ioannidis, 2005), outcome research is arguably the most biased. This is understandable because the vast majority of outcome research is conducted by those who have a very high investment—financially or professionally—in the results. But there are other problems as well. Adoption of a treatment method or medication into the evidence base is often based on a limited number of (sometimes as few as one) research studies—the one or few that support a particular point of view. However, a different picture is seen when many research studies are taken into consideration.

Brace yourself: I am about to say something that might surprise you. Though we have made great strides in the field of traumatic stress over the last decades, meta-analyses of a multitude of outcome studies covering an abundance of treatment options consistently show that *no one treatment stands out as superior to any others* (Gerger et al., 2014; Watts et al., 2013; Bisson et al., 2007; Wampold et al., 2010, among others). I already found this to be true more than a decade ago when I conducted my own meta-analysis of the outcome research on a method I have a great deal of respect for, Eye Movement Desensitization and Reprocessing (EMDR) (Rothschild, 2003). My method was informal: I read the results of all of the then currently available, published outcome studies and tracked over three columns how the outcomes fell: EMDR more, less, or the same in effectiveness in comparison to whichever method or control it was being compared to. The result was nearly equal tick marks in each column. This did not disturb me as ancedotally I knew that EMDR was very useful to a portion of my clients. But it did enlighten me to be wary of claims that one method is superior to another. I recommended then and continue to recommend that professionals should help and empower their clients to be their own best experts on themselves (as I had to do when faced with three opposing opinions for treating my IBS). In doing so, they each will be able to identify which interventions and methods help them and which do not. In addition, it is the responsibility of every trauma therapist to train and be familiar with a large variety of theories and methods so that they can adapt every course of therapy to the particular needs of each individual client.

Who Are the Trauma Therapy Research Subjects?

When considering the research, does it matter who the subjects are? You bet! Scrupulous reading of research studies of the various models of trauma therapy helps to better understand the limitations of the results. Subjects are chosen *very* carefully and selected based on many factors.

Bottom line: Researchers choose subjects who will not adversely skew the desired results (Spinazzola, Blaustein, & van der Kolk, 2005; Ronconi, Shiner, & Watts, 2014). This is particularly difficult when researching something as subjective as psychotherapy. There are just so many human variables that are unpredictable. Therefore, for example, few, if any, trauma therapy outcome studies will include clients diagnosed with personality disorders, that is unless the study is specifically looking at the effect on that population. It is also usually the case that subjects with multiple or complex traumas are not chosen for outcome studies, again, unless that is specific to the study.

The point is that trauma therapy outcome research is *not* usually based on the kinds of clients that most therapists are seeing on a regular basis. In addition, since, as mentioned in the introduction, even the most rigorous and successful studies only confirm positive results for 50% of the subjects, what of the other 50%? When an insurance company, organization, or clinic limits approved methods to one or two (which appears to be a common practice), what of the 50% or more of clients for whom those methods do not work? Based on the meta-studies cited above, it can be expected that there will be a large portion of clients who will not benefit from those methods. What are the options for them in those situations?

The Bottom Line

No study or even group of studies can ensure what works for your client. It is only the client who knows and can tell you what helps and what hurts. One of the best things any therapist can do for clients is to equip and empower them to evaluate what is useful and what is not. Then the therapy can proceed in partnership toward individualized trauma healing. These and additional concerns will be the focus of this volume.

There will be research citations periodically throughout this volume. I have chosen carefully which ones I include and which I do not. However, all should be assumed to be biased to some degree, as should the basis for my decision on inclusion and exclusion. If this was an e-mail and not a book, following the last sentence I would insert a smiley face. The purpose would be to indicate that I am admitting to my own personal and professional bias, and to underscore my disclaimer that this (and really any) book is composed of opinions rather than facts. In that way, I hope to reach way beyond the evidence base to improve the safety of trauma therapy and increase healing options for traumatized individuals of all sorts.

It is important to remember that the best expert on what helps or hurts an individual is *that* individual herself. Improving clients' skills so they are able to accurately evaluate and articulate how a therapy is affecting their body, mind, and life will go a long way toward increasing the safety and effectiveness of any phase or method of trauma treatment.

PART I

Theory and Principles

CHAPTER ONE

Revolutionizing Trauma Treatment

If you want to improve the world, start by making people feel safer.
—Stephen Porges

Trauma Recovery vs. Trauma Memory Resolution

Not long ago I received a letter from the mother of a young girl, Lisa, who had experienced much early trauma. The situation that had caused the trauma had been over for some time, but the girl continued to suffer greatly. The mother had taken her to several trauma therapists, each specializing in a different evidence-based method. Every one of the chosen therapists was highly trained and long experienced. But after trying a few sessions, every one of them sent Lisa away with the same conclusion: "I can't do any 'real work' with her because she dissociates too much." What the therapists meant by "real work" was reviewing the memories of her traumas. They felt stonewalled because when they tried to facilitate memory processing, Lisa consistently withdrew from contact.

To be honest, reading that letter sparked my ire. What, I thought, is happening to my profession? How can it be that we have become so fixated on the *memories* of trauma that we are not paying full attention to the needs of the *person* who was traumatized? To my mind, the real work for Lisa was to help her with the dissociation, *not* with the memories, and enable her to be more in control of her symptoms (dissociation among them) as well as her mind and her life. I wish that this was an isolated incident. Unfortunately, it is not. I am glad Lisa's mother wrote to me.

She reminded me that too many trauma professionals are underexposed to methods and interventions for traumatized children and adults who cannot do "real work." And it rekindled my passion for revolutionizing and redefining real trauma treatment by helping to equip all trauma therapists—no matter the methods they favor and employ—with the tools needed to *also* help people like Lisa.

Trauma Therapy Goals

Since I began studying to be a helping professional, I have always had just two goals for my career as a psychotherapist, body psychotherapist, and trauma therapist:

1. *Become obsolete.* That is, do my job well, including equipping my clients with the tools they need for self-care so that they will not need me anymore.
2. *Improve the quality of life of my clients.* This goal overrides any reliance on any one technique or theory as it is the client who will know if it is being met.

In that vein, early on I began to question being taught to do things only a certain way or to blindly accept what my teachers told me was true. Unfortunately, I increasingly noticed that following a teacher's or supervisor's directive could sometimes compromise one or both of my goals (for example, increasing client dependence in a way that was disempowering, or diminishing an individual's quality of life). My tendency to question such professional authority continues to this day. This chapter is meant to challenge the assumption that clients must process the memories of their traumatic experiences. Please do not misunderstand; I do realize that a good many do and will benefit from memory processing. Unfortunately, I have seen (and heard of) all too many resulting disasters as well. What is missing? Why is it that even with the best of intentions, many trauma clients are falling through the cracks? What other options might there be to offer them?

Historically in the trauma field, the treatment emphasis has been put on the resolution of trauma memories (Howorth, 2000; Rivers, 1918). That practice likely evolved from the psychoanalytic tradition rooted in Freud's *talking cure*. However, after working with my own clients as well as teaching, supervising, consulting with thousands of therapists, and engaging in long discussions with close colleagues, I have increasingly found the trauma therapy default mode—to process trauma memories—to be outdated and overrated. Why have therapists been taught to head first for trauma memories when it is *recovery* from trauma that our clients are seeking? Trauma recovery includes:

- Understanding that a traumatic incident is over and in the past
- Freedom from or good-enough management of symptoms, including flashbacks and dissociation
- Reestablishment or significant improvement of quality of life

Aiming first for trauma recovery never rules out the option of trauma memory resolution for those who want to tackle that. Recognizing and including trauma recovery *without* memory work as a legitimate option for trauma healing increases the treatment options for clients and therapists alike.

There is an interesting dichotomy that I have noticed among trauma therapists, trauma clinics, and developers of trauma treatment models. Many (if not most) in the trauma field hold the belief that traumatized clients must resolve all of their trauma memories in order to recover, heal, be well. Since this has never made sense to me, some years ago I began to informally poll the diversified groups of practitioners (MDs, psychologists, social workers, psychotherapists, and counselors from nearly all schools of trauma treatment and theory including cognitive-behavioral therapy, prolonged exposure, dialectical behavior therapy, EMDR, Somatic Experiencing, and so on) attending my lectures and training programs on how they have managed their own trauma healing. I do this by asking an audience (usually 24–350 participants) to raise their hands and keep them up if they:

1. Have trauma in their background
2. Have *not* worked with all of their trauma memories and resolved them
3. Have a relatively good quality of life

Invariably, by the end of my polling, one-half to four-fifths of those attending still have their hands in the air. Next, I invite them to look around to see the result themselves. Then I ask, as I do now: How can it be that we, as a profession, have become so convinced that our clients must resolve all of their trauma memories when we professionals know, ourselves, that it is not necessary?

Continuing this train of thought, the remainder of this chapter will be concerned with laying a foundation for greater attention to trauma treatment that prioritizes recovery *without* eliminating the *option* of trauma memory resolution. But first, in order to understand the difference between these two related but different goals—recovery and memory resolution—I must first pay homage to Pierre Janet and his brilliant and forward-thinking trauma treatment structure. The next section will introduce Janet's theory to lay a foundation for the discussion of recovery vs. memory resolution that follows.

Implementing Janet's Phased Treatment

Pierre Janet's *phase-oriented* structure is the gold standard for trauma treatment, no matter which method is being applied. Nearly every informed practitioner would agree that following this structure is a good idea. There is a problem, however, as it appears many are still either not familiar with it, or despite being aware of it do not adhere to it. That, despite it being prominently discussed in books and articles by van der Hart and van der Kolk as early as 1989, and many others since, including Herman (1992), van der Hart, Nijenhuis, and Steele (2006), Ogden, Minton, and Pain (2006), Rothschild (2010, 2011), and Curran (2010). Unfortunately, trauma treatment guidelines of major institutions that deal with tens of thousands of individuals with PTSD do not recommend or even mention Janet's model in their guidelines and other publications, not even the U.S. Veterans Administration (Management of Post-Traumatic Stress Working Group, 2010; Defense Centers of Excellence, 2013), National Center for PTSD (2013), the U.K. National Institute for Health Care Excellence (2005), and the International Society for Traumatic Stress Studies (Forbes et al., 2010). I found one exception in a single publication of the International Society for Traumatic Stress Studies that outlines guidelines for one specific trauma category: *complex* PTSD. In that publication, the phased model is recommended (Cloitre et al., 2012). A prominent exception, Janina Fisher (2009), has been lecturing on this topic for nearly two decades. In recent communications, we have been commiserating about how appalled we are that Janet's model is not standard operating procedure in the trauma field. By her current estimates, more than two-thirds of therapists attending her large, well-attended trainings around the world have never even heard of it. If that statistic can be generalized to the greater trauma treatment community, that is a serious information gap, indeed. A major problem is the pressure most therapists are under—from clinic administration, supervisors, insurance companies, and clients themselves—to make trauma therapy quick. While brief trauma treatment is possible in limited cases, it is not for the majority. And, unfortunately, attempts at quickening the pace can actually backfire and increase the duration. This section will outline the potential of Janet's phased structure, and its relevance to this chapter's argument to prioritize trauma recovery. Here is a brief review.

In the latter part of the nineteenth century, Dr. Pierre Janet laid a firm foundation for the future of safe trauma treatment. He defined a three-pronged system for healing from past trauma. His phase-oriented approach can be applied across the full spectrum of available philosophies, methods, and models. Simply, trauma treatment should be composed of three phases:

- *Phase 1* is concerned with establishing safety and stabilization—whether that takes hours, weeks, or even years.
- *Phase 2* involves the processing and resolution of trauma memories.

- *Phase* 3 focuses on integration, that is, applying what was gained from phases 1 and 2 into the mainstream of daily life.

Phase 1, establishing safety and stabilization, should be the foundation of all trauma treatment. The best analogy I have comes from my dear colleague, David Grill (personal communication). He likens this crucial phase to the firm and well-fitting plaster cast that is carefully constructed around a broken bone. The solidity of the cast provides safety from inadvertent twists, bumps, and jolts, as well as stability to prevent further injury. Moreover, the cast enclosure around the broken bone holds it steady and protected, allowing for the natural healing process of bone mending to occur. Without the stabilizing and safe cast properly in place, the bone may not heal properly, increasing the risk that the injured limb might never be useful again. As Grill reminded me recently, "The better the cast, the better the healing."

According to Janet, it is not advisable to move to Phase 2, working with the memories of past trauma, until the goals of Phase 1 are achieved, that is, until the traumatized individual is safe, stable, and able to function well on a daily basis. I could not agree with Janet's philosophy more and have never encountered a trauma client, professional, or author who disagreed with Janet *in principle*. However, too few actually follow this framework adequately. Those who write to me after reading my books, or attending my lectures and trainings, as well as those who seek me out for supervision and consultation, repeatedly tell me (often complaining to me) that the guidelines they are bound to follow state the processing of trauma memories as the major goal. Formally, these include the National Institute for Health Care Excellence (2005) in the United Kingdom and the Child Sexual Abuse Task Force (2004). In addition, I have been alerted to many organizations, including prominent health service agencies, that have this as an informal, though not published, policy. It is even the case (and sometimes especially) when a clinic or insurance company severely restricts the number of sessions allowed per client. Here is a typical question that I receive often, directly and via e-mail:

Many of my clients have PTSD, some with very complex histories. However, every client in my clinic is limited to 10 sessions. In addition, our treatment guidelines specify that we must work with trauma memories as the main goal of treatment. Is there any way you can help me manage these constraints with my most fragile and disturbed clients? I need help to convince my supervisor that I should be working differently with them.

Many trauma therapists are appropriately concerned and distressed that the limitations they must work under could actually be harming rather than helping their clients. Implementing Janet's phased model will, in most cases, alleviate those risks.

Applying Common Sense

Let me explain why Janet's model is so full of common sense and why it is necessary to postpone addressing trauma memories until the individual is adequately stable and safe.

There is no getting around it—recalling traumatic experiences *is* destabilizing. Opening up to memories of terror and helplessness will (less and more) unglue anyone. As a result, people who live in the aftermath of traumatic experience develop coping mechanisms, what we call *defenses*, that enable them to live with the fact of whatever it is that they have endured. Defenses may include dissociation, avoidance, repression, and so on. Some defenses will be more effective than others, but all of them help an individual to cope. Loosening defenses such as repression, avoidance, and so on, as is necessary to process trauma memories, increases instability—that is logical: When you disrupt a coping mechanism, coping becomes more difficult. *Decompensation* is the professional term for such a disruption in coping. The person loses the ability to compensate as he once was able to do.

If someone is relatively, reliably stable, it is usually safe to open the Pandora's box of trauma memory to process and make sense of what happened. That person can usually tolerate the increase in unsteadiness that results from trauma memory processing. In a Phase 2 trauma therapy, typically a client will reflect on the memory (for shorter and longer durations depending on method and client ability), moving between the destabilizing memory and the firmer ground of here-and-now reality. Stable clients can afford these dips into instability which do not, usually, compromise their ability to function (even if they do not always feel good).

However, the landscape looks different for those clients who are not stable. With those individuals, opening Pandora's box and addressing trauma memories will increase their basic unsteadiness, increasingly compromising their ability to function on a daily basis. This actually occurs often in trauma therapy. In fact, one of the articles I wrote for the *Psychotherapy Networker*, "Applying the Brakes" (Rothschild, 2004), was dedicated to just this situation: therapists leading unstable clients to process traumatic memories. The common result of those situations is further decompensation; that is, the client gets worse, sometimes a lot worse.

I have come to this point of view not only from my years working with trauma, but also from my earliest experience with neo-Reichian and other body-oriented methods that promoted strong emotional release. Many of us who were doing that type of work in the 1970s and 1980s learned the hard way that it is best to ensure a trauma client's capacity for stability and self-regulation before loosening up their capacity to feel and express emotion (Rothschild, 1993). At that time body psychotherapy was not informed by Janet, though in the years since his wisdom has been embraced quite widely in those quarters. In the same vein, common sense, as well as good judgment, serve as an important guide to the conclusion that maximizing stability *prior to* opening up to trauma memories will make any eventual Phase 2 work much safer. Clients working in Phase 2 who have a solid base of stability will be much better able to tolerate the unsteadiness of trauma memory work. They will be better able to maintain awareness of the present while processing the past, and they will be in an improved position to continue to function on a daily basis through the procedure.

Another important consideration is that not every client *wants* to reflect on their traumatic past. And as discussed above, there is no reason to believe they must or that they should be forced to do so. Some clients come to therapy knowing they want help to stabilize only. Others believe they will want to process memories but find once they become stable that the past is no longer compelling. Successful Phase 1 work can render Phase 2 work uninteresting or unnecessary.

I have heard many assert that trauma therapy consists *only* of memory processing. I could not disagree more. One of the most valuable lessons of the phased model is that *all of the phases are trauma therapy*. And, because of the importance of stabilization and safety—not just for the individual client, but also his family, his employer (or school), his community—Phase 1 cannot be overemphasized. The individual who is stable and safe, and has improved her quality of life is able to be a vitally contributing member of her family and her community.

Because of the usual treatment guidelines as mentioned above, traumatized individuals may be required to recall their traumatic experiences because it is the core of their trauma treatment. I cannot speak (and write) strongly enough against *forced* recall in the name of trauma therapy. Voluntary Phase 2 work is difficult enough under the best of circumstances and there is always the risk of retraumatization. Forced Phase 2 work is even more difficult and greatly increases the risk for retraumatization. It is worth a reminder that a key element for trauma recovery is regaining self-control. When a therapeutic authority supersedes that control by disregarding a client's wish to not remember the past, the result cannot be good. I must advocate that this too-common practice be completely eliminated from the trauma treatment field.

And what about Phase 3? Janet saw the progression from Phase 1 to Phase 2 to Phase 3 as a linear sequence. However, integration, that is, helping clients to make use of the therapy to better their daily life, needs to be a part of each phase and session of therapy. Whenever possible, I want my client to have a *takeaway* from every session. If in Phase 1, for example, we work on stopping a flashback, I want my client to hone that skill so she can use it on a daily basis to stop flashbacks that plague her regularly. When my client dissociates in the session and I help him to stabilize in the present moment, he will best be served by further helping him to do that for himself. In Phase 2 when an insight is gained, I want my client to be able to apply that new knowledge or point of view in her current life, where appropriate. Integration is a necessary part of every therapy session.

Working *in Context of* vs. Working *on* Trauma

Working in a context of past trauma involves focusing on trauma recovery while not recounting the memories. Many are now calling this *trauma informed* (Fallot & Harris, 2001; Harris & Fallot 2001). It is intimately woven with Janet's Phase 1. When working on trauma recovery, the fact that trauma has happened is not at all forgotten. Acknowledging the fact of trauma and validating accompanying symptoms is important. However, the details of the events must be put aside in favor of an emphasis on developing stability. Symptom relief and reclaiming a sense of control over body, mind, and life are the primary concerns.

In contrast, working with trauma memories necessarily involves a focus on the past. And, as previously discussed, it also necessarily involves periods of destabilization. That is the main reason why it is advisable to postpone resolution, Phase 2 work, until the client is reliably stable and safe.

Trauma Recovery

Phase 1 recovery work has as its main goal the improvement of the client's life quality on a daily basis. The focus is then, necessarily, on the here and now. Recommended tools include crisis intervention, stabilization training, supportive therapy, and mindfulness (which will be discussed at length in Chapter 8). Desired results can be seen when clients become involved (or significantly increase involvement) in their normal daily responsibilities for work, school, and home; engaging with their family, friends, and community; and working to improve health and fitness.

Though originally designed to help those with borderine personality disorder, dialectical behavior therapy (DBT) is an extremely useful adjunct for Phase 1 trauma recovery. It is filled with tools for, and practice in, stabilization and safety. For therapists feeling ill equipped to address a client's stabilization needs in Phase 1, accessing one or more books or courses on DBT will greatly enhance their Phase 1 toolbox (Linehan 1993, 2014).

Sometimes in the rush to address trauma memories in Phase 2, circumstances of life crisis can be overlooked. All of us (myself included) would do well to review what we were taught in graduate school about crisis intervention and the minimum necessities for basic human survival as outlined in, for example, Maslow's *hierarchy of needs*. All too often, the traumatized client is living in a crisis situation. In such circumstances, no amount of Phase 2 processing will put things to rights. Moreover, attempting trauma memory processing with someone who is in crisis or trauma could have dire results.

It can be challenging for both therapist and client to let memories rest in the past in the service of recovery. Janina Fisher (2009) reminds trauma professionals that listening to accounts of the past or descriptions of flashbacks are not in a client's best interest when the necessary goal is recovery and stabilization, or when a client is ill equipped to handle the dysregulation that accompanies such reports. With those clients for whom Phase 1 trauma recovery will likely be the entire therapy, letting the past rest in the past without detailing it will be a major goal.

Mindfulness is a major ally for all phases of trauma treatment, though particularly important to build a foundation for Phase 1 anchoring in the here and now. Think about it: What is PTSD? One of its major hallmarks is the pulling of one's awareness into the past via intrusive images and flashbacks: The past intrudes on the present. In contrast, the practice of mindfulness involves continually bringing awareness into *the present moment*, strengthening the individual's connection to the here and now. However, practicing mindfulness can be difficult for some with PTSD as well as those with anxiety and panic disorders. Chapter 8 will address those difficulties in detail, making mindfulness more accessible for all PTSD clients.

Another strategy that can be helpful for trauma recovery is to weaken the trauma-specific memory. This is a phenomenon that appears to occur naturally in people who have experienced trauma but have not developed

PTSD (van der Kolk, 2001; Lee, Villant, Torrey, & Elder, 1995). It seems that when traumatic experiences do not lead to PTSD, normal memory consolidation is possible. For most people, that means that as time goes by, memory of all sorts fades; it is a natural process. Memories of both good and bad events that have happened lose their sharpness as well as their punch. This normal process can sometimes be facilitated in someone with PTSD by helping him to focus on the *epilogue* to his experience (Rothschild, 2010). Basically, creating an epilogue involves paying attention to the life events *following* trauma that:

1. Affirm that the incident is over
2. Attest that the individual survived
3. Recognize that life went on

Of course, this is not true for everyone with PTSD. Some may be, for instance, continuing life under traumatic circumstances, or the events following the incident may also have been awful or included additional trauma. In such cases working with the epilogue would be contraindicated, *not* at all a good idea. However, with those clients for whom an epilogue would meet the above three criteria, it could be a useful and powerful intervention. Clinical applications of the epilogue will be further expanded and illustrated in Chapter 6.

Criteria to evaluate when individuals have recovered from trauma should include:

- Reasonable reduction of symptoms and full control over those that persist, including:
    - Ability to come out of dissociation
    - Proficiency at stopping a flashback
    - Secure skills to calm anxiety or panic attacks
- Fullfilling their life role as
    - Student
    - Parent
    - Worker

- Quality of life is felt and observed to be considerably improved
- General stress management is much improved
- Ability to distinguish trauma triggers from the actual event

Below are examples of three trauma clients who are, at least as we meet them now, most appropriate for work with trauma recovery rather than resolution.

Greg was physically and sexually abused as a child. To a large extent, he has learned to manage well and has a high-level job. However, he describes himself as fragmented. It is as if, he reports, he left a part of himself behind in his childhood. He imagines that part of him stuck in time and wants to reconnect. However, he insists that he must immediately revisit the traumatic events he endured no matter the cost.

Maryellen suffered neglect as a toddler and sexual abuse at the hands of a relative. Now at 45 she suffers from PTSD, the result of both her early experiences and a particularly traumatic medical experience three years ago. She sought therapy because she is now facing a necessary surgery and is panic stricken when dealing with doctors, medical appointments, and anticipation of the impending surgery. Her singular therapy goal is to be able to see this surgery through without going crazy.

Eric is recently returned from combat military service. He, like many of his comrades in arms, violently fought and killed as he was ordered to do while witnessing the deaths of many of his fellow soldiers. Despite a diagnosis of PTSD, he appears to function well at home and at work. However, his high-level functioning is deceptive. He reports that he has figured out how to manage his civilian life by cutting off completely from his emotions. In general, he reports feeling emotionally numb. So he functions well, but does not feel that he is really a participant in his life. He has come to therapy hoping to awaken his feelings without having to revisit his horrific war experiences.

We will take a look at all three of these clients in more depth in subsequent chapters. Greg (Chapter 3) must first gain tools for and be convinced of the advantages of stopping his flashbacks before it will be safe to connect with the traumatized part of himself he feels he left behind.

Stabilization will help Maryellen (Chapter 5) to face her surgery through the recognition and further development of resources—some she knew about, but was unable to access, and others that she cultivates anew. And Eric's (Chapter 6) emotions can be awakened just as well through exposure to powerful positive memories from his life.

Trauma Memory Resolution

Phase 2 trauma memory resolution work is focused on addressing trauma memories—preferably one event at a time. The decision of whether or not an individual should work in Phase 2 must be a joint decision of both therapist and client. The therapist needs to be responsible for safety, which includes holding back the client who wants to dive into Phase 2 memory resolution work before she has the stability and resilience necessary to make it successful. And, of course, the therapist must respect the client who does not wish to reflect on the past. However, when the client is reliably stable and safe, and therapist and client are in agreement, resolution of traumatic memories can be very beneficial.

There are many choices of *how* to resolve trauma memories in Phase 2. While in many sectors, strict adherence to the *evidence base* will determine which methods are allowable, a better strategy would be for that decision to also be between the therapist and the client. It is most advisable for therapists to each fill their professional toolbox with a variety of training methods that suit their individual styles. A minimum of three diverse methods is a good start. It is important that the therapist have multiple methods to choose from because there are *none that are suitable to all clients*. Remember, no matter how good the method—and most are very good—none work for all traumatized individuals. In an ideal setting, the therapist offers and describes two or three methods that suit his style and the client chooses the one that seems most appealing to try (or try first). Another reason why therapist skill in multiple methods is so important involves the tendency for trauma clients to go looking for the latest or most touted method they have heard about, or therapists to be hemmed in by the limitations of their clinic or own education. Never forget that the most important factor in successful therapy (also trauma therapy) is the therapeutic relationship. When therapy is hindered by limiting therapists and clients to this or that method—no matter what that method is—it cannot help but hinder the progress of many (if not most) therapies. As previously mentioned, loss of control is at the core of PTSD. So when control of the therapeutic method is taken from the client as well as the therapist, there is greater potential for relationship ruptures.

Nonetheless, varying methods each have their own mechanism, though all have features in common. Some methods aim to desensitize the memory through repeated exposure; others process memories in short segments; there are those that work more with resolving trauma's effect on the body; and all—in one way or another—seek to heal how trauma impacts the mind and psyche. (For a longer discussion and comparison of numerous various methods of trauma therapy, see *Trauma Essentials* [Rothschild, 2011].)

How long it takes to resolve a trauma memory will depend on many factors. But assuring that adequate time has been spent on establishing safety and stabilization in Phase 1 will ensure a shorter and more manageable course of therapy. Time and again, consultation on cases where Phase 2 work is going badly (dissociation, decompensation, hospitalization, and so on) reveals that Phase 1 work was either bypassed or shortened in favor of jumping to memory resolution. Usually this happens under pressure to shorten a therapy course. Particularly in clinics where the number of trauma therapy sessions is greatly limited, both therapist and client often feel urgency to advance to working with memories. It would be a huge benefit to all if the administrators making those decisions realized that giving more time to Phase 1 and Phase 3 would actually save time in Phase 2.

Recognizing successful resolution of trauma memories includes:

- The memory of the trauma is no longer triggering; that is, recounting the narrative of the event does not result in hyperarousal, dissociation, or the like.
- Symptoms associated with the trauma memory and PTSD have abated.

- Avoidance of reminders of the trauma are no longer an issue.
- The client is fully engaged in "normal life."
- The client's nervous system recovers easily (normally) from every-day stress.

It cannot be emphasized enough that, despite the advantages of successful Phase 2 trauma memory resolution work, those same advantages evaporate when memory resolution is attempted either prematurely or against the will of the client.

Who might be most appropriate for trauma memory resolution work?

Peter, a war veteran, watched as his best friend blew apart from stepping on a landmine. Despite effective stabilization work and reliable support from his family and friends, he does not feel finished. He has learned to stop the intrusion of the mental images (see "Controlling Images" in Rothschild, 2003), but he feels he would benefit further from confronting the memory and excising the associated emotions. At his local Veterans Administration hospital, the therapists mostly work with the cognitive-behavioral method of prolonged exposure. Peter feels ready to face his memories with that method.

Gabrielle was raped by a stranger when she was at university. She coped well in spite of her ordeal. She finished her studies, went on to a successful career, and became a wife and mother. Her own daughter is taking off for college in a year, and Gabrielle sought therapy when delayed-onset PTSD hit. She was panicked at the idea of her daughter living on her own in a dormitory or apartment where Gabrielle could not look out for her. Phase 1 has gone well. She understands the difference between herself and her daughter and is able to apply dual awareness effectively. Nonetheless, she feels that she would be in a better position to let her daughter live her own life if she processed her memories and left them more securely in the past. Eye Movement Desensitization and Reprocessing (EMDR) is the method she feels will be most helpful to her.

Donna and her family survived the 2004 Indian Ocean tsunami. They were there on vacation when it struck. For a period of over 12 hours she was in panic and chaos until she was able to locate and gather everyone together. Despite the fact they all survived, she could not let go of the fear and feeling of impending doom. Phase 1 work has been effective and she does recognize the difference between now and then. However, she continues to feel overprotective of all family members and that is overflowing into her daughter's marriage and the birth of her first grandchild. She believes that by revisiting her memories of the tsunami she will be able to recognize in her mind as well as her body that it was a singular event so she can stop fearing that another such tragedy will take her family and her grandbaby from her. Strongly body oriented, Donna chose Somatic Experiencing to process her trauma.

Past vs. Now and Future

As you may now have surmised, the choice between working with trauma recovery or trauma memory resolution has much to do with whether the desired focus is on the present or on the past. And while it may seem obvious, I would like to take a deeper look into this. The short answer here is that there may be more value in the one or the other at a particular point in time. However, as I discussed in the introduction to this book, we as a profession may have put too much importance on the past and I will take this opportunity to put forward an argument for my point of view.

Truth be told, the past is stable. What happened, happened. No matter what we do in therapy—or even on an esoteric or spiritual level—no one can change history. How it is remembered, how it is reported, how it is felt or interpreted, how we regard it, and different viewpoints can all change, but the facts of the past are permanent. We cannot change the past, no matter how hard we try or how good our tools. It is just not possible. The past is, literally, out of our reach, out of our control. Period. Full stop.

The good news is, we can change the *effect* the past continues to have on ourselves and our clients now and in the future. That is really the aim of both trauma recovery and trauma memory resolution. However, some therapies place—I believe—an unbalanced emphasis on reviewing the past, often repeatedly. That may result in desensitization to the memory of the past, but may not address the effect the trauma has on the person in daily life and into the future.

There are several approaches that are particularly good at paying attention to trauma's effect now. As mentioned before, mindfulness practices and DBT are particularly geared for this in Phase 1 work. For Phase 2 resolution work, Peter Levine's *Somatic Experiencing* and Francine Shapiro's EMDR are particularly designed to target the *current effect* of past trauma. Somatic Experiencing does this by teaching the client to track her present-moment responses to a trauma memory, paying particular attention to body sensations, muscular impulses, emotions, and thoughts—not those of the past, but the ones occurring *in the moment*. EMDR addresses the current effect through a particular aspect of the protocol where the client also pays attention to current emotion and body sensations, and—what I think may be the core of EMDR's success— what they call the *negative cognition*. The EMDR therapist will (among other things) ask the client, "When you remember [the event], how do you feel about yourself *now*?" Then the next question is, "How would you rather feel about yourself?" In that way, the EMDR therapy nails how the past trauma continues to effect the client's self-concept and at the same time lays the foundation toward a more healthy self-concept as the therapy progresses.

Making Meaning From Trauma

As discussed above, PTSD takes root not because of what happened, per se, but because of how the effect of the trauma continues to adversely impact the individual's life. What is the point of trauma therapy, whether it is trauma recovery or trauma memory resolution? Certainly symptom reduction and, as mentioned before, improving quality of life; in addition, integrating what is learned in the process and being able to apply that learning to leave the traumatic event in the past and also make a better future. A major route to those goals is through making meaning out of the traumatic experience. In fact, it has been shown that making meaning through gaining the sense of a higher purpose is an important dynamic in trauma recovery (Alim et al., 2008). This is a significant part of what Janet intended from including Phase 3, *integration*, in his structured model.

Making meaning from trauma can include gaining a greater understanding, changing a point of view, what is often called an "ah ha!" experience, and so on. It often involves changing what the trauma means to the person with PTSD. And while working with the meaning is usually thought of as being a part of Phase 2, it is also possible, where appropriate, as a part of Phase 1. Below are examples of each: a Phase 1 application from marriage and family therapist Charley Lang and a Phase 2 application from Dr. Peter Levine.

Making Meaning in Phase 1 Therapy

In a recently published article, narrative therapist Charley Lang (2016) deftly demonstrates how meaning can be made of traumatic events and their aftermath without having to review the details of the incident. In fact, when the client, Jake, comes for his first session and announces, "I'm finally ready to do it . . . tell . . . all the gory details" of being abused, Lang kindly but firmly stops him in his tracks. Interestingly, the start of this session is quite similar to the one I will recount in Chapter 3 with my client, Greg. These are *not* the same client, but the coincidence is a good reminder of how common it is for a trauma client to arrive expecting, needing, or fearing he will be required to tell his trauma story in detail— no matter the consequences. It is actually the fact that Lang knew to dissuade his new client from following a one-size-fits-all approach that piqued my interest to read further. And I'm glad I did! Prior to reading this article, I had never considered how potent narrative therapy could be for helping a trauma client, particularly in Phase 1.

Instead of targeting the details of the traumatic event, Lang focused on the *effects* the trauma had on Jake's life. The resulting feeling of shame became the focal point of the therapy. Eventually, Jake was able to assert that the shame he had been feeling and hiding actually belonged with the abusers, not with himself. Simultaneously, Lang and Jake began to identify resources that may have been lost to Jake because of the abuse. In exploring both themes, shame and lost resources, "Slowly, a distinction begins to emerge . . . between the identity description enforced by shame and Jake's own preferred sense of himself in the world." This formed the basis for shifting how Jake thought of himself. As a result, gradually his life quality improved as his traumatic past took a back seat to his improving self-concept and a more hopeful present and future. Jake then became proactive in altering the meaning of his life by engaging in volunteer work he had considered for a long time, but previously shied from.

Last, Lang helped Jake to further change and enhance meaning by asking him to name someone from anytime in his life who would be cheering for his inner and outer changes. Jake was able to name a particular schoolteacher who had seen and supported his potential early on. In this way, together therapist and client reawakened an important past resource (see Chapter 5 for an extended discussion of resources) and strengthened Jake's internalization of that teacher and his support.

Lang's case is an excellent example of how the meaning and effect of trauma, as discussed in the pages above, can be changed in a present moment–anchored Phase 1 therapy.

Changing Meaning in Phase 2

In *Waking the Tiger*, Levine (1996, pp. 112–119) recounts a workshop therapy session with a young Greenlander named Marius. There are many dimensions to this story and therapy session, and I highly recommend reading it in its entirety. However, in keeping with the current topic under debate, I will be limiting my discussion to the meaning aspect of the therapy. (And just for historical reference, I was present at this session, which took place during the first workshop I attended with Levine. The timing was good for me since it was in Copenhagen shortly after I moved there in 1988.)

The reason Marius asked for the therapy session was, he said, because he tended to get anxious with men whose approval he sought. As he explored this issue a particular memory emerged as important. As a boy, Marius had been savagely attacked by a pack of wild dogs, coincidently on the same day his mother had given him his first pair of hunter's trousers made by her from polar bear fur—an important and proud milestone. As he first recounted the traumatic incident, he described being carried home in an injured and bloody state by a neighbor who had found him. He remembered his father coming to the door of their house and perceived him as looking annoyed. That perception had a big effect on Marius. The meaning he made of it was that his father was angry and rejecting him. As a result, Marius felt very hurt as well as angry himself.

Levine proceeded to help Marius with the method he now calls *Somatic Experiencing*, working with Marius's body as well as his thoughts and feelings. Part of the therapy involved Marius imagining being able to attack the dogs himself. In doing so he actually ripped a roll of paper towels to shreds. As he claimed and reclaimed a feeling of power in his body, emotions were expressed. At last he again remembered being carried home, but this time the images—and the meaning—changed. When he remembered his father this time. Marius saw that his father was not angry, but scared and worried. With this realization, the meaning of the incident changed and Marius cried with relief: "I'm okay and he was just scared. It's not that he doesn't love me" (Levine, 1996, p. 117).

Levine would likely argue that it was the careful and precise body work that resolved the traumatic memory. I would agree that this was integral. But we might disagree on what really resolved the issue. The way I see it (and saw it at the time) is that the *change in meaning* is what led to resolution. Of course it is possible that other aspects of the therapy were necessary to enable Marius to change his perception, but it is still the new meaning that made it possible for him to lay the memory to rest.

In Chapter 4 you will find a transcribed therapy session with Una (p. 96) that further illustrates the importance of making meaning. Toward the end of that session, following a significant emotional catharsis, Una has a realization. She has been pushing herself to finish grieving too quickly and is finally able to see she "must learn to take smaller steps." It is with that realization that she makes a leap toward resolving her issue.

In conclusion, remember that prioritizing trauma recovery is all inclusive. Anyone recovering and securing reliable stabilization and safety always has the option to process and resolve trauma memories. But it does not work the same in the opposite way. Prioritizing trauma memory resolution too often bypasses or shortchanges Phase 1 stabilization and safety, and can result in further dysregulation, anxiety, flashbacks, and dissociation. People in these situations may feel compelled to seek trauma memory resolution continually and unendingly. To prevent such a risk, securing a firm base via Phase 1 work will go a long way toward ensuring the safety and success of Phase 2 memory processing.

CHAPTER TWO

Precision ANS Regulation

What to Look For

Everything in physiology follows the rule
that too much can be as bad as too little.

—Robert M. Sapolsky

Three or so decades ago, one of my clients, Greta, after much preparation, was ready, we agreed, to process memories of a very traumatic childhood incident. This was the first time she had wanted to talk about it and I was interested. Too interested. We both became so engrossed in her account that it was only when she was finished that either of us realized something had gone terribly wrong. Rather than feeling better from the telling, she was extremely anxious and so stiff she could barely move. During the next week she was plagued with panic attacks and called me multiple times for support and stabilization. For her, what should have been an exciting progression in her therapy backfired into regression.

In another situation, a new client, Hans, easily answered all of the usual intake and assessment questions and told me he was "fine." Nonetheless, when he left my office he became very confused and lost his way several times on his familiar route home. He was so distressed that he canceled the next appointment we had scheduled and never returned.

Could I have prevented these therapeutic disasters? I believe so. In those days I was brand new to traumatic stress studies and had not yet been exposed to theory or tools that would have helped me to monitor autonomic nervous system (ANS) arousal. I wish that I had that knowledge then. Likely, I would have noticed as Greta's facial expression gradually lost its animation, her respiration quickened, and her skin tone slowly blanched. Those observations would have led me to slowing down or stopping her narrative, *putting on the brakes*, to reduce arousal and stabilize before she went on. It might even have meant pacing her memory processing in a different way, taking it slower and in smaller pieces. Likewise, with the necessary information and greater understanding, I might have seen that Hans was *not* "fine," that his pupils were dilating. I could have inquired about the temperature of his hands and feet, and I may have noticed as his posture became more collapsed.

Nevertheless, I did learn from those costly mistakes and, as a result, became interested in knowing more about identifying the effects of ANS arousal. My observational skills gradually improved—for example, for a long time I just could not see changes in skin tone, but did eventually with persistence. And I learned, as well as created, interventions for *putting on the brakes*. Consequently, the therapy I provided became safer and more digestible for my clients and, as a side effect, my own professional balance benefited from self-observation as well.

Such experiences piqued my interest in passing on what I learned about making trauma treatment safer through observation and modulation of the ANS. Therefore, the purpose of this chapter is to review and then update and integrate current understanding and observation of the ANS. In particular, I aim to give trauma therapists a new and improved tool that they can use to gauge and monitor their clients'—*and their own*—level of autonomic arousal at any given moment in time. By doing so, therapists will always be in the position to know whether their clients are able to safely manage what is happening and if they are able to integrate what is being worked on in therapy. Likewise, the therapist will also know if she herself is able to think clearly despite the level of stress in herself and her client. To this end, I want to expand your knowledge of *what to look for* and what to do about what you see and hear from the client, as well as what you sense in your own body. There is a full-color insert following page 66 that contains one table and one chart that will be fully explained within this chapter. I hope they will contribute to the understanding of ANS arousal states so that clients can be better monitored, evaluated, and regulated.

You may want to take your time with this chapter. Many of my colleagues read earlier versions of it, helping me to better explain the concepts and make it more accessible without diluting it. Nonetheless, it is dense. Do not be concerned if you need to read it more than once to grasp the particulars.

At least where the treatment of trauma is concerned, there needs to be a great deal of precision in the therapy, perhaps even more than with other types of counseling and mental health issues as in the examples, above, of what can go wrong. You have probably already encountered the volatility of trauma treatment. Clients can easily get triggered, come unglued, and flip into flashback and other types of dysregulated states. That is because traumatized individuals are prone to extreme disruptions of their nervous systems which can sometimes lead to unpredictable emotional and somatic responses. ANS arousal levels can suddenly skyrocket or plummet, causing enormous discomfort, threatening emotional stability, and risking retraumatization. On the emotional side these responses may include anxiety, panic, dissociative episodes, confusion, and flashbacks. Examples of bodily disruptions can consist of extremely high or low heart rate or blood pressure, palpitations, hyperventilation, fainting, and the like. Over the last few decades, multiple methods for helping individuals recover from traumatic incidents have been developed. Though they emerged from divergent disciplines, these methods all have at least two things in common: structure and precision. To heal trauma, many in the field of traumatic stress have independently discovered that a therapist must be able to monitor and direct the process at all times. That includes being able to quickly identify when ANS arousal is at a safe or dangerous level, and then having the knowledge and tools to quickly intervene to maintain emotional and physical safety as well as optimal integration of the treatment process where required.

To assist with the care necessary for effective and responsible trauma treatment, more precise tools are required to help practitioners in their work. They need to be able to assess the client's state of nervous system regulation from minute to minute, and repeatedly intervene to keep ANS arousal within manageable levels. Moreover, the therapist must constantly observe his own internal state lest a trigger, vicarious trauma, or countertransference overactivate his own nervous system. If that happens, it could render him incapable of the clear thinking necessary to conduct safe, precise, and effective trauma therapy. *No matter which method of therapy or trauma treatment you are using, being able to track your client's and your own arousal level will make the therapy safer for you both.* In this chapter, I hope to clarify questions such as:

- When is arousal at a level where integration is possible?
- How will I know when my client is on the verge of a freeze state so that we can avoid it?
- When is it okay to continue what we are doing in the therapy?
- What would indicate it is time to put on the brakes?

Bottom line: The goal is to keep both the therapist and client thinking clearly and able to integrate and make sense of what is happening throughout the entire therapy session. First and foremost, that will help to ensure that the therapy is safe. In addition, monitoring ANS arousal will lay a foundation for optimum effectiveness of the therapy and achievement of short- and long-term goals.

Reviewing the ANS

The body's nervous system is understood as divided into multiple parts. The two main branches are the central nervous system (brain and spinal cord) and the peripheral nervous system, which contains the motor and sensory divisions. The sensory nervous system will be discussed in depth in the next chapter. The motor division is made up of nerves that communicate from brain to body (efferent) to stimulate muscles including the somatic part that activates skeletal muscles, those that move bones (such as bending your leg), and the autonomic part (the topic of this chapter) that regulates the viscera and visceral muscles such as the heart, lungs, and stomach. Below is a simple chart that illustrates these relationships (see Figure 2.1).

Figure 2.1. The body's nervous system.

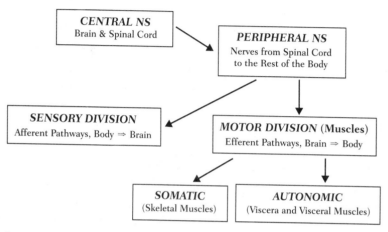

© 2000, 2016 Babette Rothschild

Autonomic Nervous System: The Basics

The ANS was first named at the turn of the 20th century (Langley, 1903). Since that time, it has been widely acknowledged in physiology and neuroscience to be composed of two distinct branches: the *sympathetic nervous system* (SNS) and *parasympathetic nervous system* (PNS). It has been commonly accepted that SNS activation is involved in states of stress, from mild activation to the extremely aroused responses associated with threat: flight, fight, and freeze. The PNS, on the other hand, is most activated in states of rest and restoration. At times the SNS has also been referred to as *excitatory* or the *accelerator*, and the PNS as *inhibitory* or the *brake*. These two branches usually work in balance, like the arms on a scale of justice—when one rises, the other suppresses and vice versa. When, for example, the SNS is predominantly activated, the viscera and visceral muscles will be stimulated to send large amounts of oxygen to the muscles for quick and strong movement. That is why SNS arousal is characterized by increases in pulse and respiration, and also the reason that the mouth goes dry (no need for digestion when speed and strength are the priorities). Primary activation of the PNS is different. In that state the main concern is to send blood flow to the digestive system to absorb nutrition and to the skin to keep the body warm. To accomplish that, pulse and respiration slow, and the nervous system becomes calm. This simplified understanding of the ANS has been applied for more than a century. It is this theory that I learned when I was first studying the neurophysiology of trauma. While it makes sense and is useful to a point, it is also limiting.

Background

In my first book, *The Body Remembers*, Volume 1 (Rothschild, 2000), I began a discussion of *what to look for* in clients in order to increase the safety and precision of trauma treatment through more accurate regulation of ANS arousal. In that book, I adapted a fairly typical table for understanding the ANS. These types of tables are readily available in nearly every physiology book and in the images section of an online Google search. As is usual, that one has two columns, one for each of the two acknowledged (at that time) ANS branches: parasympathetic (PNS) and sympathetic (SNS). The observable characteristics listed under each branch reflected the most accurate indicators that were known and speculated at the time of the book's publication, gleaned from basic physiology texts and the then most recent work of Peter Levine (1992, 1997) and Gordon Gallup (1977). It is reproduced below (see Figure 2.2).

In addition to that table, some pages later, I suggested guidelines for recognizing progressive states of arousal, from "relaxed" to "endangering."

- *Relaxed system:* primarily moderate activation of parasympathetic nervous system (PNS). Breathing is easy and deep; heart rate is slow; skin tone is normal.
- *Slight arousal:* signs of low to moderate PNS activation combined with low-level sympathetic nervous system (SNS) activation: breathing or heart rate may quicken while skin color remains nor-

Figure 2.2. Autonomic nervous system (smooth muscles) (involuntary).

SYMPATHETIC BRANCH	PARASYMPATHETIC BRANCH
Activates during positive and negative stress states, including: sexual climax, rage, desperation, terror, anxiety/panic, trauma	States of activation include: rest and relaxation, sexual arousal, happiness, anger, grief, sadness

Noticeable signs

  Faster respiration
  Quicker heart rate (pulse)
  Increased blood pressure
  Pupils dilate
  Pale skin color
  Increased sweating
  Skin cold (possibly clammy)
  Digestion (and peristalsis) decreases

Noticeable signs

  Slower, deeper respiration
  Slower heart rate (pulse)
  Decreased blood pressure
  Pupils constrict
  Flushed skin color
  Skin dry (usually warm) to touch
  Digestion (and peristalsis) increases

During actual traumatic event OR with flashback (visual, auditory and/or sensory)

Preparation for quick movement, leading to possible fight reflex or flight reflex

During actual traumatic event OR with flashback (visual, auditory and/or sensory)

Can also activate concurrently with, while masking, sympathetic activation leading to tonic immobility: freezing reflex (like a mouse, caught by a cat, going dead). Marked by simultaneous signs of high sympathetic and parasympathetic activation.

mal; skin may pale and moisten slightly without increases in respiration and pulse, etc.

- *Moderate hyperarousal:* primarily signs of increased SNS arousal: rapid heart beat, rapid respiration, becoming pale, etc.
- *Severe hyperarousal:* primarily signs of very high SNS arousal: accelerated heartbeat, accelerated respiration, pale skin tone, cold sweating, etc.
- *Endangering hyperarousal:* signs of very high activation of both SNS and PNS, for example: pale (or reduced color) skin (SNS) with slow heartbeat (PNS); widely dilated pupils (SNS) with flushed color (PNS); slow heart rate (PNS) with rapid breathing (SNS); very slow respiration (PNS) with fast heartbeat (SNS), etc. (Rothschild, 2000, p. 111)

I received much positive feedback on the table and the guidelines. However, useful as these tools were, I was aware that there were still many situations that were not yet understood.

Over the last decades, I and my colleagues and students have done our best with what we had, but I always hoped that such a basic table could be bettered. However, until recently, I was just not sure how. And then, a couple of years ago, while updating multiple training program handouts, some "bricks" fell into place. I realized that some of the missing pieces might be filled in by *adding* important points from the alternative ANS theory proposed by Stephen Porges (2001, 2011). Many in the fields of traumatic stress studies, psychotherapy, and body psychotherapy have fully embraced Porges's *polyvagal theory*. My position is sort of middle-of-the-road. I see value in *both* the old and the new theories. Porges's view *adds* to and betters our ANS knowledge, but is not a complete replacement for the traditional views. This is one of those areas where, as mentioned in my disclaimer, disagreement fuels growth. No matter which side of the debate your opinion falls on, I hope you will be open to considering the advantages of a synthesis of the two rather than having to adhere to one or the other. Particularly with regard to my goal for this chapter, that is, sharpening the therapist's ability to observe and monitor the client's nervous system arousal—as well as to monitor his own arousal—integrating Porges's theory with the standard ANS theory is a huge advantage.

Porges's Polyvagal Theory

Steven Porges (2001, 2011) has made the single most progressive contribution to the understanding of the autonomic nervous system in recent times. There is a lot to this theory, enough to warrant a book of over 300 pages. As a result, there is no way I will be able to discuss it in its entirety in this brief chapter. I will, therefore, be focusing on the points I have found most relevant to trauma treatment.

Porges's major theory concerns identification of separate actions of two distinct complexes of the vagus nerve on the ANS: the *ventral* branch (at the front of the body) and *dorsal* (at the back of the body).

His theory has helped both researchers and practitioners to make better sense of what is happening in individuals when they are calm (ventral vagus) and when they collapse under the most extreme stress, threat to life (dorsal vagus).

Porges's theory challenges and expands the traditional scientific understanding of the ANS (per the chart previously discussed above). He has proposed that the vagus nerve has two separate branches that operate in distinctly different ways on the ANS. In his view, activation in the ventral branch of the vagus nerve associates to the action of the calming aspects of the parasympathetic nervous system. When the parasympathetic, ventral vagal, is most active, the nervous system is in a mostly calm state. Critical to Porges's theory, it is important to note that also in such a state, social engagement, that is, contact with self and others, is most possible.

On the other end of the spectrum, Porges ascribes activation in the dorsal branch of the vagus nerve to the extreme trauma response of flaccid-muscle freezing. He sees this dorsal-vagal freeze as a hypoaroused state connected to an excessive activation of the parasympathetic nervous system. The result is a dramatic shutdown of traumatic hyperarousal which leads to immobilization and collapse.

Reconciling the Old With the New

I, like many of my colleagues, have been struggling to reconcile and integrate these overlapping but differing views of ANS function for many years. I endeavor to view them as complementary rather than conflicting. And, primarily, I want to extract the most vital information from each to increase my understanding of what I see and hear when I am working with a client (and also sense in myself). To that end, I have completely revised and expanded the traditional ANS table. In doing so, it has become a new tool that can be employed to enhance the precision and safety of trauma treatment. I recommend using it to simultaneously monitor a client's and therapist's ANS arousal. The aim is to make possible a more nuanced and better-regulated treatment for the client and the reduction of adverse events for both therapist (vicarious trauma, compassion fatigue) and client (overwhelm, collapse, retraumatization).

Sextuple ANS Theory

Those older ANS tables that assign the characteristics of the two branches, the SNS and the PNS, are very limiting for those who work with traumatized individuals on a regular basis. To be able to precisely monitor clients and themselves, practitioners need to be able to identify a greater range of nuance that distinguishes levels of arousal *within* each of those branches. For example, PNS activation, which is usually thought of as a good thing—calm and restorative—can actually be dangerous if the PNS activates too high, and it can be very draining if the arousal goes too low.

In the hopes of solving many of the aforementioned ANS table problems (or, at the least, making a significant contribution in that direction), the following table represents an updated and integrated representation of the organization of the ANS. The best way to view it is in full color on the glossy foldout following page 66. I suggest that you put a placeholder of some sort with the table so that you can easily refer to it and follow along as the details are explained. Within the text I will reprint the line or column from the table that is under discussion so that you can see what I am talking about. However, those will be in black and white. You will need to refer to the table itself to see the associated color scheme being described.

The main purpose of this table is to help practitioners to specifically identify *what to look for* when observing ANS states in clients and in themselves. For the client this will mean increasing opportunities to reduce or even (eventually) prevent dysregulation, catching a rise in arousal *before* it gets out of control. For the therapist, it will make it possible to more accurately monitor her own arousal so that she can ensure her ability to think clearly and prevent vicarious trauma. The table also provides general guidance on how to intervene therapeutically depending on what is observed. Here it is in black and white:

How to View This Table

With this table I am hypothesizing six distinct (though overlapping) degrees of ANS arousal, three levels each within SNS and PNS: SNS

AUTONOMIC NERVOUS SYSTEM: PRECISION REGULATION
** WHAT TO LOOK FOR **

	Yellow	Green	Blue	Orange	Red	Purple
	LETHARGIC Parasympathetic I (PNS I)	**CALM** Parasympathetic II (PNS II) Ventral Vagus	**ACTIVE/ALERT** Sympathetic I (SNS I)	**FLIGHT/FIGHT** Sympathetic II (SNS II)	**HYPER FREEZE** Sympathetic III (SNS III)	**HYPO FREEZE** Parasympathetic III (PNS III) Dorsal Vagus Collapse
		← "Normal" Life →			Threat to Life	
PRIMARY STATE	Apathy, Depression	Safe, Clear Thinking, Social Engagement	Alert, Ready to Act	React to Danger	Await Opportunity to Escape	Prepare for Death
AROUSAL	Too Low	Low	Moderate	High	Extreme Overload	Excessive Overwhelm Induces Hypoarousal
MUSCLES	Slack	Relaxed/toned	Toned	Tense	Rigid (deer in the headlights)	Flaccid
RESPIRATION	Shallow	Easy, often into belly	Increasing rate	Fast, often in upper chest	Hyperventilation	Hypo-ventilation
HEART RATE	Slow	Resting	Quicker or more forceful	Quick and/or forceful	Tachycardia (very fast)	Bradycardia (very slow)
BLOOD PRESSURE	Likely low	Normal	On the rise	Elevated	Significantly high	Significantly low
PUPILS, EYES, EYE LIDS	Pupils smaller, lids may be heavy	Pupils smaller, eyes moist, eye lids relaxed	Pupils widening, eyes less moist, eye lids toned	Pupils very dilated, eyes dry, eye lids tensed/raised	Pupils very small or dilated, eyes very dry, lids very tense	Lids drooping, eyes closed or open and fixed
SKIN TONE	Variable	Rosy hue, color (blood flows to skin)	Less rosy hue (blood flows to skin)	Pale hue, despite skin color (blood flow to muscles)	May be pale and/or flushed	Noticeably pale
HUMIDITY Skin	Dry	Dry	Increased sweat	Increased sweat, may be cold	Cold sweat	Cold sweat
HUMIDITY Mouth	Variable	Moist	Less moist	Dry	Dry	Dry
HANDS & FEET (TEMPERATURE)	May be warm or cool	Warm	Cool	Cold	Extremes of cold & hot	Cold
DIGESTION	Variable	Increase	Decrease	Stops	Evacuate bowel & bladder	Stopped
EMOTIONS (LIKELY)	Grief, sadness, shame, disgust	Calm, pleasure, love, sexual arousal	Anger, shame, disgust, anxiety, excitement, sexual climax	Rage, fear	Terror, may be dissociation	May be too dissociated to feel anything
CONTACT WITH SELF & OTHERS	Withdrawn	Probable	Possible	Limited	Not likely	Impossible
FRONTAL CORTEX	May or may not be accessible	Should be accessible	Should be accessible	May or may not be accessible	Likely inaccessible	Inaccessible
INTEGRATION	Not likely	Likely	Likely	Not likely	Impossible	Impossible
RECOMMENDED INTERVENTION	Activate, Gently Increase Energy	Continue Therapy Direction	Continue Therapy Direction	Put on Brakes	Slam on Brakes	Medical Emergency CALL PARAMEDICS

*Observe client states: To modulate arousal with brakes. Adjust in yourself: To think clearly & prevent vicarious trauma & compassion fatigue.

© 2000, 2014, 2016 Babette Rothschild   Sources: Multiple medical & physiology texts; P. Levine, 2010; S. Porges, 2011

I, II, III and PNS I, II, III. The left-to-right color scheme is inspired by both the United States' and United Kingdom's terror threat warning-level posters. They both use green to represent low or no threat, blue to stand for a state of guarded alert, orange to mean high alert, and red to warn of the most imminent severe threat. In the sextuple-ANS theory, those colors are used to indicate four of the graduated phases of ANS arousal response (see the horizontal row labeled Primary State). Yellow has been added to the far left column and purple to the far right column. Detailed explanations will follow.

	Yellow	Green	Blue	Orange	Red	Purple
PRIMARY STATE	Apathy, Depression	Safe, Clear Thinking, Social Engagement	Alert, Ready to Act	React to Danger	Await Opportunity to Escape	Prepare for Death

Yellow indicates a state of arousal that is too low, a type of *hypoarousal*, though this low-energy state is *not* the result of traumatic stress. Green represents the ANS in a state of safety and calm. Blue designates the rise in arousal that is needed to meet the demands of daily life. Orange represents arousal response to perceived or actual threat that one can fight or flee. Red indicates an activated freeze state that may, eventually, allow escape. Purple specifies the most dire situation when threat of death appears to be imminent and complete overwhelm results in collapse, which is a second (and more recognized) type of hypoarousal. (The two types of hypoarousal will be discussed in more depth below.)

With this new table I am hoping to resolve difficulties and fill in gaps that are not addressed with the standard two-column ANS chart. As discussed above, the SNS and PNS are activated, to varying degrees, in both desirable and undesirable states. For this reason, I have added labels at the top of the table, one to indicate that the arousal levels of PNS II and SNS I are associated with *normal daily life* and that SNS II, SNS III, and PNS III are associated with *threat to life*. That appears as below in the table:

	Yellow	Green	Blue	Orange	Red	Purple
	LETHARGIC Parasympathetic I (PNS I)	CALM Parasympathetic II (PNS II) Ventral Vagus	ACTIVE/ALERT Sympathetic I (SNS I)	FLIGHT/FIGHT Sympathetic II (SNS II)	HYP*ER* FREEZE Sympathetic III (SNS III)	HYP*O* FREEZE Parasympathetic III (PNS III) Dorsal Vagus Collapse
		⟨— "Normal" Life —⟩		⟨— Threat to Life —⟩		
PRIMARY STATE	Apathy, Depression	Safe, Clear Thinking, Social Engagement	Alert, Ready to Act	React to Danger	Await Opportunity to Escape	Prepare for Death
AROUSAL	Too Low	Low	Moderate	High	Extreme Overload	Excessive Overwhelm Induces Hypoarousal

People with normally regulated nervous systems and life situations routinely swing between low and moderate levels of arousal depending on whether they are at rest (eating and digesting, hanging out with friends, sleeping) or are mildly stressed with everyday kinds of situations or demands (cleaning house, meeting a deadline, running a race, having sex) and so on. The stress of moderate challenges such as conflict with a spouse or a work dilemma would usually fall within the blue SNS I. It is only during exceptional situations where there is a threat to life or limb that an individual moves into higher arousal states represented by the orange SNS II (*high*), red SNS III (*extreme overload*), and purple PNS III (*excessive overwhelm*) columns. It is these *rare* situations that we call *traumatic*. Arousal in the *threat-to-life* range dysregulates and pushes the ANS to the reactions of flight, fight, and freeze. On the other end of the spectrum, the yellow PNS I column represents a state where arousal is too low to function well. Depression, apathy, lethargy, chronic fatigue, and such would fall into this category. The PNS I column does not fall under either the "normal life" or "threat to life" banner because it does not qualify; it is a state unto itself.

I am hoping that dividing the SNS into three stages of increasing arousal will clarify some of the confusion about how the SNS could be involved in both desirable kinds of stress (such as having sex) and likewise in the most horrible types of incidents (such as assault). Identifying three levels of SNS arousal helps to distinguish these differences. It can also help a therapist to notice when arousal is on the rise and may be moving into a zone that could threaten her own or the client's clear thinking, or worse. Likewise, dividing the PNS into three stages should help to illustrate the extreme difference between desirable PNS II activation and life-threatening PNS III activation.

Of course the lines and colors dividing the columns are not meant to represent rigid boundaries. And within each column the range of arousal can vary. For example, within the blue column might be response to demands that require very little arousal, say working in the garden, to situations that stimulate fairly high, though not hyperarousal, for example a failed house sale or dealing with major plumbing problems. That overlap and progression are represented in the row labeled Primary State by the rainbow graduation of color changes throughout the six columns from yellow at the far left to dark purple at the far right. You will note, for example, that the color in the blue SNS I column fades from greenish-turquoise at the left of that column through pure blue in the middle to a darker blue mixed with a little orange at the right.

Keeping with the goal of the chapter, that is, guiding helping professionals in *what to look for* to be able to gauge arousal in clients and themselves, each column includes a list of typical physical states (on the buff-colored background) that coincide with each level of arousal. Look, for example, at the row labeled Heart Rate:

	Yellow	Green	Blue	Orange	Red	Purple
HEART RATE	Slow	Resting	Quicker or more forceful	Quick and\or forceful	Tachycardia (very fast)	Bradycardia (very slow)

Slow pulse in PNS I yellow, resting pulse PNS II green, and the quick or forceful pulse when threat is involved indicates SNS II orange. Scanning across the row labeled Integration in the cognitive and emotional states section (on the light gray background), you will see:

	Yellow	Green	Blue	Orange	Red	Purple
INTEGRATION	Not likely	Likely	Likely	Not likely	Impossible	Impossible

This means you can anticipate when your client is calm (green) or moderately activated (blue) that cognitive integration will likely be possible, and so on.

Likewise, each column indicates probable observable physical, cognitive, and emotional states associated with that level of arousal. Read down the orange Flight/Fight Sympathetic II column:

The primary state is *reaction to danger*; arousal is *high*; muscles are *tense*, and so on down the column. The bottom row includes a *recommended intervention*, which in this case is to *put on the brakes*. In the same way, each column highlights the characteristics associated with that arousal level. When looking at your client, or monitoring your own internal state, observations that primarily fit in the one column or

	FLIGHT/FIGHT Sympathetic II (SNS II)
PRIMARY STATE	**React to Danger**
AROUSAL	**High**
MUSCLES	Tense
RESPIRATION	Fast, often in upper chest
HEART RATE	Quick and/or forceful
BLOOD PRESSURE	Elevated
PUPILS, EYES, EYE LIDS	Pupils very dilated, eyes dry, eye lids tensed/raised
SKIN TONE	Pale hue, despite skin color (blood flow to muscles)
HUMIDITY — Skin	Increased sweat, may be cold
HUMIDITY — Mouth	Dry
HANDS & FEET (TEMPERATURE)	Cold
DIGESTION	Stops
EMOTIONS (LIKELY)	Rage, fear
CONTACT WITH SELF & OTHERS	Limited
FRONTAL CORTEX	May or may not be accessible
INTEGRATION	Not likely
RECOMMENDED INTERVENTION	**Put on Brakes**

another will guide you in identifying current arousal level and also give you a recommendation for how (or if) to intervene.

Two Categories of Freeze

It is generally agreed that when faced with threat to life, both animals and humans assume a *state of freeze*, that is, the organism becomes completely muscularly immobile, with diminished awareness. For a long time, it has been believed that the freeze state is a single condition (Gallup, 1977), even though in some situations the immobility appears with muscle stiffness and in others with muscle flaccidity. However, increasingly in the last decade or so, I and some of my colleagues have been wondering if there might be *two* functionally different states of trauma-induced freeze. Porges (2011) has certainly contributed to the understanding of the flaccid muscle collapse. But what about the stiff muscle paralysis? I have represented two possible differing states of freeze in the red SNS III column, indicating a hy*per* freeze state where muscles are rigid and heart rate is very fast, and the purple PNS III column representing the hypo freeze state where muscles are flaccid and heart rate is very slow. Because differing actions of the PNS are involved in the yellow lethargic, green calm, and the purple hypo freeze/collapse states, they are distinguished as PNS I, PNS II, and PNS III respectively.

It is believed that traumatic freeze states serve at least two purposes. *Hyper freeze*, in the red SNS III column, is common in the wild when, for example, a deer or kangaroo becomes stiff in a car's headlights or a predator catches up to its immobilized prey. Hyper freeze appears to be a survival strategy since a stiffly motionless prey might appear to the predator to be dead. *If*, as a result, the predator then abandons the prey, it may have a chance to quickly revive and escape. The other type of freeze, *hypo freeze* in the PNS III purple column, may serve as a preparation for death by dampening consciousness and reducing perception of pain. The PNS III hypo freeze state is also sometimes referred to as *hypoarousal*.

Let me give you examples of how these two states of freeze might look in the therapy room. But first a caveat: It is best to avoid freeze states altogether as they are not therapeutically beneficial. When clients' activation goes that high, they are seriously at risk for retraumatization, decompensation, and even, possibly, actual death. This is a major reason why monitoring the ANS is so important, to be able to catch and reduce arousal before it rises to such a dangerous level.

Clients in (or approaching) an SNS III hyper freeze state will become immobile from tensed muscles. (Think of my client, Grete, described at the beginning of this chapter.) They may look stiff in the chair. Their facial expression will become decreasingly mobile; breathing will become more rapid; and their pupils will dilate. They may be able to respond to questions, but thinking will not be clear. In this situation, the best response is to *slam on the brakes*. That is, do whatever you can to reduce stress and provocation. That might mean insisting on contact with exteroceptors (per the next chapter), or, perhaps, moving your chair to give more space. Firm reassurance that the client is with you and not at the scene of the trauma should also help.

First responders and those who work in hospital emergency rooms will likely see someone collapse in a PNS III state, but it is rare during trauma treatment. I have never witnessed this in therapy myself. The only situations I am aware of where hypo freeze has occurred during trauma therapy were the result of clients being forced to face memories of near-death experiences without any preparation, grounding, resourcing, development of therapeutic relationship, and so on. Hopefully, that means that anyone practicing even the bare minimum of safety precautions will likely avoid such a calamity. However, it is certainly possible, depending on where you work, that an individual could arrive in the immediate aftermath of, for example, a car accident, being raped, a shooting, and so on. In that type of circumstance, hypo freeze is definitely possible. You will recognize this dangerous situation if the client collapses or faints with muscles flaccid (instead of stiff). If you check the pulse, you will likely find it *very* slow. Hypo freeze immobility is actually a potentially life-threatening situation. The only responsible intervention is to call for paramedics and remain with your client until they arrive.

The understanding of hypoarousal does not stop here. In the next section I will be proposing that there are two distinct categories of what is often referred to as hyporarousal.

Two Types of Hypoarousal

I have a confession: For a long time I rejected Dan Siegel's (1999) concept of a *window of tolerance* because everything I read, saw, and heard in discussions confused me. Generally, hypoarousal has been thought of as one thing, a collapse that is the result of dorsal-vagal stimulation, an extreme PNS arousal. I do agree with that and have represented this state in the purple PNS III column. Despite the knowledge that such a collapse was the result of some kind of extreme threat to life, the commonly recommended intervention has been to stimulate and energize the collapsed person in an effort to bring him or her out of that state. That recommendation has never made sense to me and I have seen it have adverse results. If someone is collapsed in terror, completely overwhelmed, why add more provocation? Recently, another of those bricks fell into place. I realized that there may be a confusion between the low energy of PNS III collapse and a lethargy or withdrawal that might result from chronic (though *not* traumatic) stress, depression, bereavement, apathy, and the like. So here is another hypothesis: There are *two* distinct types of hypoarousal. The one is, as described above, the result of over-the-top PNS III traumatic arousal that causes a possibly life-threatening collapse. In addition, there is a second type of hypoarousal that is *not* the result of trauma, but is akin to apathy or lethargy, perhaps a kind of giving up. I have represented this non-trauma-related hypoarousal on the ANS table in the first, PNS I yellow, column.

There is a critical difference between the low energy of someone who is very sad, aggrieved, or depressed, and the state of hypoarousal collapse that may occur during or in the immediate aftermath of a life-threatening event or, more rarely, in one suffering from severe PTSD. The first one, PNS I, is the result of a deficit of energy. PNS III hypoarousal is, on the other hand, the result of overwhelming arousal which causes a nervous system shutdown that leads to collapse. PNS III hypoarousal is the result of arousal going *over the top*. Thinking in those terms will help you to distinguish that as a state of excessive overwhelm rather than an absence of vigor.

Here is a computer analogy that will help to make this distinction. I am going to compare the PNS III hypo freeze state of hypoarousal to the all-too-common computer crash. A computer crash can occur for a myriad of reasons, the three most common are:

- Too many programs or applications running at the same time, overwhelming the operating system.
- The hard drive becomes too full, causing overload.
- An electrical surge blows out the system or precipitates a protective shutdown.

Consider the PNS III hypoarousal collapse as similar. Neither is the result of too little arousal, energy, or movement. They are both precipitated from *too much* of something. In the case of the computer, it is too much data or electricity. PNS III hypoarousal collapse follows SNS III hyperarousal when the threat becomes so intense that death may be imminent. Neither of these situations (human or computer) will be eased by increasing activity, load, or charge. You would not want to further overload an already overloaded computer system. What the computer needs is some sort of reduction in activity, data, or electricity. Likewise, for PNS III hypoarousal, someone in that condition needs a *reduction* in the level of provocation and threat that they are under, feeling, or perceiving, not more.

PNS I hypoarousal, the one that stems from a lack of verve, is more akin to a computer battery that has lost charge or a slowdown because the Wi-Fi signal has dropped off. In these cases, some kind of energy boost would be necessary and appropriate. The same goes for lethargic people. Increasing their energy would be in order, so long as it is gentle and well-paced (Brantbjerg, 2008).*

One critical key to differentiating between these two states of low energy is to pay attention to what, exactly, *preceded* the hypoarousal: Is the person tired? Is this the result of a chronic or acute depression? Or, instead, has arousal been on the rise? Has the person just experienced a traumatic event? Was there provocation from a trigger or an episode of flashback? These are among the important questions to be asking before choosing an intervention. The PNS I state needs gently increased stimulation; PNS III requires reduction in stimulation. It will also be critical to note if the person is conscious, in contact, has fainted, and so on. In the case of fainting or losing consciousness, check the pulse. Is it fast or slow? A reminder: If this is a hypo freeze collapse, the safest intervention is to call the paramedics.

To further illustrate the difference between these two types of hypoarousal, I have drawn a second view of the ANS table on its side and have integrated some of the concepts from the *window of tolerance* proposed by Daniel Siegel (1999) and popularized by Pat Ogden and col-

---

* Merete Holm Brantbjerg has an understanding of, and skill in working with, the lethargic, low energy, state like no one else to my knowledge. I highly recommend this rare article as there is nothing even close to it available, at least that I could find.

Figure 2.3. Window of affect tolerance and integration.

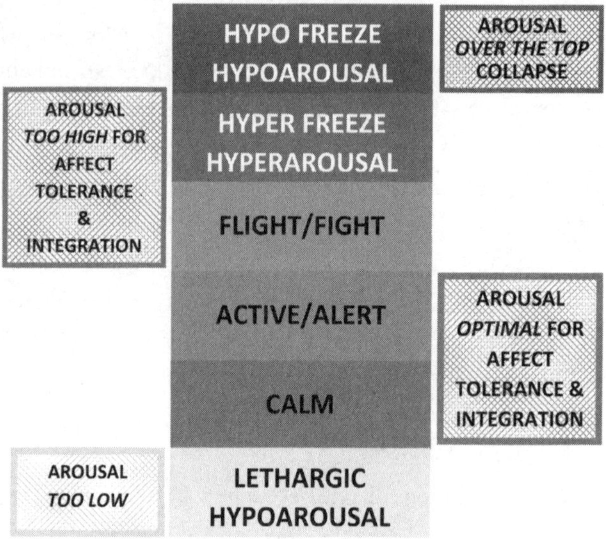

© 2016 Babette Rothschild; Adapted from Siegel (1999) and Ogden (2006)

leagues (2006) (see Figure 2.3). A full-color version of this table is also viewable on the glossy insert following page 66.

As you can see from this chart, hypo freeze hypoarousal *arises* from increasing threat and arousal until those become so massive and severe that the body collapses, literally *over the top*. On the other end, the lethargic hypoarousal state is, literally, on the low end of the arousal scale. In that instance arousal is just too low.

Emotions and the ANS

Reading across the Emotions (Likely) row, you will notice that most of them are assembled into the yellow PNS I, green PNS II, and blue SNS I columns. This is because the usual range of human emotions (sadness, pleasure, love, shame, disgust, anger, anxiety, and so on) coincides with the lower ranges of ANS arousal. Rage, fear, and terror are all extreme emotions that are associated with the more highly stressed states of orange SNS II, red SNS III, and purple PNS III.

	Yellow	Green	Blue	Orange	Red	Purple
EMOTIONS (LIKELY)	Grief, sadness, shame, disgust	Calm, pleasure, love, sexual arousal	Anger, shame, disgust, anxiety, excitement, sexual climax	Rage, fear	Terror, may be dissociation	May be too dissociated to feel anything

I had the greatest difficulty, as well as the most colleague discussions and online searching, in placing the emotions of shame and disgust. For the first, there is little discussion or research on the association between emotions and the ANS. Those who research the neurophysiology of emotion appear to be more concerned with what is happening in the brain than in what it feels or looks like in the body. Therefore, this is an area where anecdotal and personal experience had to be my main guide. Consensus among my colleagues gleaned from client and self-observation as well as the limited available literature led to the conclusion that disgust and shame had features of both yellow PNS I and blue SNS I. Perhaps when I am or someone else is ready to update this table, there will be additional or clearer research to guide more accurate placement of these emotions.

How to Use This Table

Each of the six levels of ANS arousal is represented by separate columns. Reading from left to right, the level of arousal increases with each step: PNS I, PNS II, PNS III, SNS I, SNS II, SNS III, and PNS III. Likewise, when reading from right to left, arousal is decreasing. Down the left side of the table are listed common features that, in varying degree, help to evaluate which arousal level is currently active. Physical indicators are on a light yellow background, and cognitive and emotional indicators are on a light gray background, for example, if you read down the list of features to the indicator of Muscles then follow that across the columns to the right:

	Yellow	Green	Blue	Orange	Red	Purple
MUSCLES	Slack	Relaxed/toned	Toned	Tense	Rigid (deer in the headlights)	Flaccid

Under the heading of yellow PNS I the muscles will likely be slack; in green PNS II the indication is that muscles in that state will be relaxed; under the heading of blue SNS I, muscles will be toned; when the arousal is at the orange SNS II level, muscles will likely be quite tense; and when arousal is extremely high—inducing a state of freeze—the muscles could either be very rigid (red SNS III) or completely flaccid (purple PNS III).

When the physiological, cognitive, and emotional indicators on this table are committed to memory, it becomes possible to quickly identify what is happening in a client and in oneself. (However, do not worry if memorization of this sort is not in your skill set. You can always refer to the table.) Some of the characteristics are easy to identify through visual observation: nuances of skin tone (no matter the base color of a person's skin), variations in pupil size, and differences in breathing patterns. Others require inquiry (asking clients if they can identify the speed of their pulse, feel the temperature in their hands and feet) and listening for which emotions are being named or expressed during the session. In this way the table can become a treatment tool of value to aid modulation of the therapy session, keeping the pace and stimulation within parameters that the client can manage and integrate. Likewise, learning these characteristics and how they feel in your own body will make it possible to monitor your own arousal level, enabling you to keep it in a range where you are alert and able to think clearly.

Something as detailed as identifying ANS characteristics can be difficult to weave into already demanding situations of trauma treatment. Changing your therapeutic routine to include attention to such factors can be challenging. When I was first learning to identify ANS signs in my clients and myself, I had particular difficulty remembering to notice what was happening. I solved that hitch by taking a file card and drawing a big ANS on it in bold red letters. I stuck it on the wall behind the chair where my clients usually sat. It was hard to miss and helped to remind me to check on my own and my client's ANS arousal during sessions. Most clients ignored my sign. But a few asked what it meant or what it was for. The discussion that then resulted was usually rich for the client and for me. We furthered a stronger partnership as the clients also gained knowledge and skill in identifying ANS arousal in themselves. And once in a while one would surprise me with an observation of my arousal state! Unnerved at first, I became accustomed to and eventually looked forward to my clients being able to gauge my arousal. It meant they had gained a tool for themselves to use, not only in the session, but in their daily lives as well. Not a bad idea to be able to gauge the arousal in another, for example, while confronting a difficult issue. For many that can be very empowering. And, periodically, I would introduce the ANS to a client who had not noticed the sign because it seemed she might benefit from that bit of knowledge. If dealt out in digestible portions, it can be useful information for just about anyone.

Once you are able to identify the current state of a client's (or your own) arousal, you will be in a much better position to intervene to modulate the arousal level. Often (but not always) that could mean *putting on the brakes*, slowing things down, grounding, and so on to reduce arousal to a lower, safer level, one where clear thinking is optimized.

I have now presented and taught versions of this updated ANS table to a good many groups of trauma therapists during large training lectures and smaller training programs around the world. The response has been exceedingly positive. From the anecdotal feedback I have received to date, it appears this new ANS table facilitates a more accessible and useful conceptualization of what a therapist sees in a client and observes in herself. Trainees have spontaneously begun to describe their own and client states within the color scheme:

- "I am feeling mostly in the green right now, calm and clear thinking."
- "Now I understand that my difficult client is mostly in the orange during sessions. That must be why he is not remembering what we did."
- "When I am working I am usually moving between green and blue."
- "What do you do for a client who suddenly shoots into the red?"

In this way, they have told me, they can much better see the differences between arousal levels, and immediately understand the meaning because of the color associations. And more than one psychiatrist has told me they wished they had such a clear and comprehensive tool in medical school.

Making Sense of Monitoring the ANS in Practice

I know from my own experience that no matter how accessibly presented, learning and digesting the complexities of the ANS can be a lot to absorb, organize, and remember. In an effort to help with that, below I will narrate an example of what putting this knowledge to use might look like in practice.

My client, Jennifer, arrives late. She seems in a rush and her skin tone is pale and her pupils are dilated. When she sits I can see her breathing is shallow but quick. Her muscles are tense and shaking and she looks ready to bolt from her chair. Upon inquiry, she responds that she is feeling "very scared."

These are signs of high arousal, corresponding to the Flight/Fight orange SNS II column. I do not dare ask her what is upsetting her as I predict that either she would be unable to reply or that encouraging her to think about what is distressing her could drive her arousal even higher. I decide to help her *put on the brakes.* I first fall back on my "go to," which is to encourage mindful body awareness and ask what she notices in the hope that paying attention to her body sensations right now will help to ground and calm her.

In a quavering voice Jennifer tells me that her hands and feet are cold. But when I ask about her heart rate, she becomes unable to speak and just pats her chest rapidly to show me that it is beating fast. Though her face remains pale, her ears begin to flush.

Of course, no intervention or strategy works for everyone, nor even every time with the same person. I become concerned that asking about her body has driven her arousal even higher. She is now edging into the hyper freeze, red SNS III state. Sometimes using body awareness can be a way to gently put on the brakes, but not always. In this instance, that strategy has further destabilized her. I realize that if I am to prevent her from becoming completely frozen, I must *slam* on the brakes using a different strategy. Since body focus increased her dysregulation, I decide to move away from that and have her turn her attention to me and the room, drawing on her exteroceptive sensory system (per Chapter 3), helping her to focus outward rather than inward.

I ask Jennifer to identify the color of my hair, the time on the clock, and the number of flowers in the vase. In addition I direct her to notice the noise outside the window. She is able to follow all of these directions. As she does, her breathing starts to slow, she sits back in her chair, and her tense shoulders drop slightly.

These responses tell me her arousal is easing back to orange SNS II and starting to move toward the Active/Alert blue SNS I. Not there yet, but on the way.

Encouraged, I ask Jennifer if I am doing anything that is frightening her. She tells me no, "but you must not come closer."

The fact of that considered reply tells me that she is becoming able to think clearly and speak in her own defense. That indicates she is even more into the blue SNS I than I had realized.

I want to take advantage of her increased clarity and ask if I should move my chair back to give more space between us. She tells me she doesn't know if it matters, but it might be good to try. When asked how far I should move she indicates about one foot (30 centimeters). Once I have scooted backward, she takes a long breath and exhales deeply, almost like a sigh. I draw her attention to this and she affirms, "It's easier to breathe when you are not so close."

That deeper, slower breath also tells me that her arousal has come way down, fully in the blue SNS I and on the way toward the green PNS II of calm. We work in a similar vein for a few more minutes until I can see by all somatic indicators that she is, indeed, PNS II calm (green), and that she experiences that also. It is useful for Jennifer, as for most traumatized individuals, to be able to experience what calm actually feels like. Some have forgotten; others have rarely, if ever, experienced calm. Developing a *somatic marker* (Damasio, 1994; see Chapter 6 for a detailed discussion) for calm is like establishing a safe home base. She will now know what to aim for to be able to think clearly and function better.

This process has taken up merely the first 8 minutes of the session. With her nervous system calmed and her cortex fully available, she is now in a good position to be able to make sense of what was distressing her when she first arrived. We agree to address this and I continue to monitor her arousal in the same way, keeping her as much as possible in the green PNS II calm and blue SNS I active/alert areas (calm and moderate arousal) so that she can make use of and integrate what we are discussing.

Periodically, while working with Jennifer (and, hopefully, all of my clients) I am also monitoring my own arousal levels. It is important that I keep my own activation in check, in the green PNS II calm and blue SNS I active/alert areas so that I, too, can think clearly. If I let myself become overly activated, dysregulated into flight/fight SNS II orange or worse, I will not be of any use to my client. Further, I could risk vicarious trauma or decompensation myself, neither of which would do me (or my client!) any good at all. Likewise, if I succumb, for example, to tiredness or grief over a recent loss, I could sink into the PNS I lethargic state where clear thinking is also compromised. So when I am checking on Jennifer's arousal, I'm also, at least some of the time, checking on my own as well. When she first arrived in that distressed state, I could feel my own heart rate go up and my hands cooled. As she calmed, my pulse slowed and my hands warmed up, so I knew I had resonated with her distress and then was calming as she did. It is not always the case that the therapist's arousal level will mirror the client's, though it is a common phenomenon. This is one of the reasons to monitor yourself. If my client's arousal had not come down, it would not do either of us any good for mine to also remain high. I would need to intervene with myself to reduce the resonance (which will be discussed in Chapter 8) so that my arousal level would reflect my own state and not my client's. However, the therapist can become triggered in his own traumatic past (many, if not most, trauma therapists are wounded healers), another reason for keeping tabs on one's own state. It can be critical for keeping one's personal history contained and out of the way of the client's therapy.

Summary

Though the tables and hypotheses discussed here are concerned with observable parameters, they have not been confirmed through rigorous research. Nonetheless they are still clinically useful. As stated in the disclaimer at the beginning of this book, these are my best, current approximations. I hope that I and others will continue to improve on them. There are many topics discussed in this chapter that could benefit from further study.

Paying attention to arousal levels per the ANS table and intervening to maximize calm and integration will ensure that a client is able to maintain contact and relationship with himself and with the therapist—a prerequisite for safe trauma treatment.

When working with traumatized individuals, I am always tracking and then regulating what is happening in the ANS of my client and myself. The same goes for all of the illustrative demonstration sessions that are transcribed and annotated in subsequent chapters. Where appropriate, I will include those observations in the notes that accompany those transcripts.

CHAPTER THREE

Safety Requires *All* the Senses

Sensory Stabilization

Nothing can cure the soul but the senses.
—Oscar Wilde

Post-traumatic stress disorder (PTSD) results, in large part, from loss of the ability to recognize the present as different from the past. It is primarily characterized by intrusive memories in the form of images (visual, auditory) and distressing body sensations that are reminders of overwhelming, life-and-limb-threatening events. These unbidden memories can be so intense (*flashbacks*) that they can fool the mind and nervous system into believing that the past event is essentially happening again in the present. When that happens, somatic reactions often mirror the body's response during the actual event. As a result, those who suffer from PTSD become vigilant for *triggers* that elicit such reactions, often confusing a trigger with the original event and losing their ability to hold a normal *dual awareness* that distinguishes the present from the past (Rothschild, 2000). The key to recognizing, managing, and correcting this loss of dual awareness lies in understanding the function of the *sensory nervous system*—an often-neglected area of PTSD study, theory, and treatment. The development of a secure dual awareness is a necessary part of stabilization and safety (Janet's Phase 1) and a vital prerequisite to trauma memory processing (Janet's Phase 2). Eventually, a well-developed capacity for dual awareness will aid integration by relegating trauma memories to their proper place in personal history where they belong (Janet's Phase 3).

The preceding chapter on the autonomic nervous system presented, among other things, a comprehensive table for aiding the therapist's ability to monitor a client's ANS state through multiple levels of arousal including those related to various degrees of threat. The bottom row of that table indicates *recommended interventions* for managing the various arousal states that can occur in a client (and also the therapist) during a trauma treatment. When arousal reaches the SNS II orange, flight/fight level the instruction is to "put on brakes," and when it rises to the red SNS III hyper freeze level, to "slam on brakes." Both of those guidelines imply the need to help clients to quickly reduce the intensifying overload of provocation dysregulating their nervous systems. There are numerous strategies for lessening an extreme degree of arousal, many of which are described in my previous books as well as books of many others. However, one of the quickest, most reliable, and least utilized routes to stabilization is via connecting clients with their sensory nervous system, particularly the exteroceptive branch.

Despite advances in the theory and treatment of PTSD, including growing acceptance of the vital role of the body in traumatic stress and trauma recovery—and my own best efforts (Rothschild, 2000, 2010)—one of the more neglected areas of study and practice in the field of traumatic stress continues to be the sensory nervous system. I cannot emphasize strongly enough the wealth of knowledge, principles, and interventions to be garnered from in-depth understanding of this area of neurophysiology. Once absorbed, application from the theory and principles will make it possible—among other things—for you to help your clients to:

- Phase 1: *quickly* and *reliably* stabilize dysregulated states of anxiety, dissociation, panic
- Phase 1: *efficiently* stop flashbacks
- Phase 1: *consistently* distinguish past from present, including differentiating reactions to trauma triggers from actual trauma recurrence
- Phase 2: *confidently* maintain awareness of the present moment while simultaneously remembering what happened in the past

- Phase 2: *increasingly* identify and implement current and past resources to antidote the terror of past trauma

Though seemingly complicated, you may be surprised just how simple it can be to anchor your client in the *present moment* by the use of the sensory nervous system, something that is commonly elusive for those with PTSD (to be discussed further in Chapter 8). The theory, principles, and tools presented in this chapter will support and further the phased model discussion begun in Chapter 1, for the benefit of both trauma recovery and trauma memory resolution.

In order to equip you with the necessary knowledge and tools to accomplish the feats mentioned above, I will first briefly review basic theory of the sensory nervous system and then extract the most relevant principles. Finally, the theory and practice will be tied together by demonstrating application of the relevant principles in an annotated session transcript.

Structure and Function of the Sensory Nervous System

This chapter expands on the discussion of the body's nervous system begun in the previous chapter by focusing on the *sensory nervous system* (see Figure 3.1). The sensory division of the body's nervous system is made up of nerves that communicate from the body to the brain (afferent) by stimulation of the senses (hearing a sound, noticing the sensation of hunger). There are two classes of senses distinguished in this part of the nervous system. One is the exteroceptive, which is made up of nerves that connect to the environment external to the body. The other is the interoceptive, which connects to the environment inside of the body. *Exteroceptors* are usually referred to as the "five senses": sight, hearing, smell, taste, and touch.* *Interoceptors* are nerves involved in balance (the vestibular sense)

---

* I am aware that in recent years some authors and teachers have begun to refer to "seven senses," classifying together those that are exteroceptive and the ones that are

Figure 3.1. The Body's Nervous System

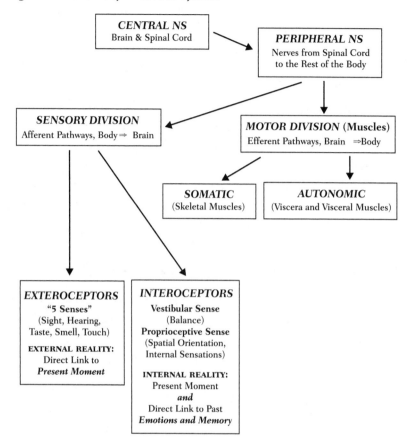

© 2000, 2016 Babette Rothschild

and proprioception, which includes the internal sense (such as feeling your heart beat or butterflies in your stomach) and spatial orientation, the ability to find your body in space (making it possible, for example, to walk without looking at your feet).

Interoceptors gather information from the inside of the body. They are the direct link to the emotions and body as well as emotional mem-

---

interoceptive. At least for my purpose here, stabilizing PTSD, distinguishing these two separate branches of the sensory nervous system is important.

ory. Focusing on interoceptors, for example, sensations in the stomach or the feeling of a rapid heartbeat, helps an individual to know his present-moment internal experience. It is also through such a focus that emotions can be identified and memory can be evoked. In fact, much of traumatic memory is composed of highly unpleasant body sensations that are experienced via the interoceptive nerves, both at the time of the traumatic events and upon recall. It is through the interoceptors that the *trauma-tainted perception of internal reality is formed*.

Exteroceptors gather information from the environment external to the body. It is through the exteroceptors (what is seen, heard, smelled, tasted, and touched) that the perception of *external reality*, that which is occurring in the present moment, is formed.

Enabling Balance in the Sensory Nervous System

In previous books I've discussed and promoted the concept of *dual awareness* in the sensory nervous system, that is, achieving a balance between perception of the exteroceptors and interoceptors—external reality and internal reality. While people with well-regulated nervous systems are able to accomplish this routinely, it is elusive for those with PTSD. It is my view that PTSD is (in large part) a failure of dual awareness, which leads to:

- Overreliance on, and hypervigilance for, distressing *interoceptive* cues
- An inability to recognize the present as *different* from the past

People with PTSD are usually all too aware of their internal sensations. That is understandable as these are the usual source of most of their PTSD symptoms. It is via the interoceptors that a client will often be overwhelmed by a collection of highly unpleasant and disabling bodily signs that tell them something is drastically wrong. Those include episodes of speeding or irregular heartbeat, digestive disorders (irritable bowel and others), balance disturbances (e.g., vertigo), intrusive auditory or visual imagery (including flashbacks), and so on. Their internal experience is a constant reminder of PTSD. They are often so overwhelmed by the disturbing interoceptive input of their internal reality that they mistake it for external reality. This results in jumping to conclusions or judgments about the environment based on interoceptive experience rather than evaluating the actual circumstances via exteroceptors. They do not look, listen, and smell to identify or locate danger. Instead they *assume* there is danger because they are feeling scared. People with PTSD are less likely to use their exteroceptors to evaluate external reality. This results in at least two major difficulties. Not using exteroceptors to evaluate the external environment means:

1. Never actually knowing when a situation is safe
2. Never actually knowing when a situation is dangerous

It is commonly acknowledged among trauma professionals that those with PTSD have a susceptibility to becoming traumatized again. In the literature this is discussed as *learned helplessness* or the defense mechanism known as *repetition compulsion*. Although these probably contribute to this phenomenon, I believe there is more to it than that. When someone is habitually focused on interoceptive experience and not much in touch with exteroceptors, the chance of missing environmental dangers skyrockets.

Of course, interoceptors are also very important. Among other things, they help the body stay upright and give valuable information about the state of internal organs and such. Interoceptive information forms the basis for our sense of self. However, it is not a good idea to be focused on interoceptors while, for example, driving a car or doing house repairs. The problem in PTSD is *not* the interoceptors, per se, but the *imbalance* of attention toward the interoceptors and away from the exteroceptors. During my professional trainings I often assign attendees to go off in pairs to walk around (the building, the garden, wherever is available at the venue) while one of them shifts focus between exteroceptors and interoceptors for about a minute each as the other makes sure to keep her partner out of harm's way. The idea is to give them a taste of what it might be like to be absorbed solely in one sensory system or the other. The feedback consensus is that immersion in interoceptors while moving around in the world feels rather dangerous and that attention to exteroceptors feels much safer.

Dual awareness (Rothschild, 2000), balancing attention to both interoceptors and exteroceptors simultaneously, is a valuable skill, though it can take some time to develop through the therapy process. Until that facility is reliable, however, there is a readily available shortcut to stabilization that is reached merely via exclusively focusing on the exteroceptors. Even with a brand-new client, before there is a therapeutic contract or alliance, directing the client to concentrate on exteroceptors, that is, simply attending to one or two for just a moment at a time, will help a dysregulated, distressed client toward (if not to) a calmer state. Even when clients have flashbacks, persistently directing them to pay attention to their external environment via exteroceptors (What do you see? Hear? and so on) will boost their connection with the here and now. Helping a client to stabilize by accessing exteroceptors is, at the same time, equally easy and difficult. The pull of the past and of internal distress can be extremely strong. To be able to quickly and repeatedly help with that, the therapist must be willing and able to interrupt as well as persevere.

Many therapists question the appropriateness of interrupting clients in their narrative, or even during an out-of-control emotional outburst. Many psychotherapy educational programs encourage following clients in their process and never stopping them. However, at least when dealing with PTSD, it can actually be dangerous to allow or encourage destabilized and dysregulated clients to continue in such states when they are unable to stabilize and regulate on their own—a common reason many seek treatment in the first place. It is therefore necessary for the therapist to interrupt the client. (And I will be demonstrating this, liberally, in the session transcript that follows below.) To be able to interrupt sometimes requires that the therapist contains his own curiosity about the narrative, resisting interest in or the seduction of the client's trauma story. The effort will be worthwhile. Not to do so would be like letting an automobile drive without any control or brakes (this is exactly the disaster that occurred in the session with Greta that I described at the beginning of Chapter 2). When the therapist interrupts and directs a client whose process is out of control, it benefits them both. In so doing, the client will be able, gradually, to learn to regulate herself. In turn, interrupting an uncontrolled and uncontained process will help the therapist reduce his own risk of vicarious trauma.

It is also very common for a therapist to direct clients to pay attention to their internal experience. That makes sense as symptoms are usually noticed through the interoceptors (heart, digestion, aches, dizziness, and such). Of course that is appropriate and helpful when a client is stable enough to explore that territory. However, when a therapy is primarily focused on internal experience, important information and stabilization tools might be missed. Helping a client to steady via exteroceptors may require both therapist and client to modify certain long-held points of view, change habits, and try new tacks in this regard. But the result can be hugely rewarding. One of my own trainees reflected exactly that to me in a poem she wrote following the first 4-day module of a 12-day training. Clare Jones told me it is the first poem she has ever written and that she was inspired to write it following that workshop, which included a lengthy unit on the importance of exteroceptive attention. Clare told me that the sensory nervous system module reawakened an important resource for her. She gave me permission to print her poem, "I Am Free," at the start of this book. It movingly illuminates the value of being able to access and focus on exteroceptors.

Even when a client cannot reliably access and hold exteroceptive attention, it is still worth the effort for brief periods of time. Of course, it is important to include clients in this strategizing, explaining the advantages of exteroceptive attention and even, perhaps, experimenting with it before achieving a focus in this direction. Persistence will steadily build facility in connecting to exteroceptors and thereby external reality, the here and now. But even before that facility is developed, checking in with exteroceptors will give a client's highly aroused nervous system a break, temporarily calming it down. That makes possible a sort of "reboot" so when the climb in arousal begins again, it is from a lowered starting point. When therapists are not persistent in holding client awareness in the present moment via exteroceptors, the risk for retraumatization increases. However, often this is not easy to do. In the next section an annotated session transcript will demonstrate these principles.

Accessing exteroceptors is also useful for the helping professional herself when working with clients or attending workshops, conferences, and trainings on PTSD. It is quite normal for professionals to get triggered by a client's process or a difficult topic of discussion into their own traumatic past—after all, most of us in this field are wounded healers ourselves. When that happens, particularly in those situations, it is *not* a good idea to focus on one's internal experience, which usually leads to increased unsteadiness. Instead, the professional needs to stabilize herself in order to be available to the client or to make use of the learning opportunities.

First Session Stabilization: Greg

The case that follows is based on a video demonstration that I often show during professional training programs. Regardless if the audience is large or small, when, after watching the video, I ask how many therapists in the audience have had a client like this, nearly every hand is raised. Therefore, I expect that most readers will find something familiar and helpful in this illustrative initial therapy session.

This is the challenge: Greg is a brand-new client appearing for the first session. He repeatedly dissociates or slips into flashback, making it impossible for me to obtain any history, make an assessment, or discuss his needs and goals. Basically I have three choices:

- Let the client stay in the dysregulated state hoping he can find his way out on his own.
- Refuse to work with the client, as did the therapists mentioned in the example at the start of Chapter 1.
- Or, alternatively, I could work determinedly to stabilize this client even if only for short bursts at a time.

I will choose the third option and invest in this client by helping him to regulate his nervous system and get anchored in the here and now. Of course, that is not easy to do—even less so with this client who is so determined to tell his trauma story in detail no matter the cost.

It is my aim that by the end of this chapter you will have gained confidence to stick with stabilizing this type of client.

Greg: Stabilizing a New Client

Greg is in his early 40s. This is the first therapy session. I know from the initial phone contact that he was sexually abused as a child and is coming because the degree of dysregulation he deals with on a daily basis is disrupting his ability to manage a normal life. This session is usually reserved for assessment and history taking—that is, a complete history, not just trauma (see discussion in the next chapter for expansion on this). But as we begin the session, I can already see that history taking is not going to be possible during this session. Greg is both determined and obsessed with launching into his story of abuse. The more he is drawn into his memories, the more distressed and dysregulated he becomes. Therefore, in this case I must alter my usual goals. The first aim is to help Greg to stabilize and keep his awareness in the here and now, away from his memories of the past.

> Therapist [T]: Hello, Greg. This is the first time we are meeting. As we discussed on the phone, I have some questions to get to know you. . . .
>
> Greg [G]: [interrupting while taking a big breath] Here we go, here we go, this is it. I'm gonna do it.
>
> T: You're gonna do what?
>
> G: Talk about it.
>
> T: Oh, not yet. I'd like us to get to know each other, first.
>
> G: I want to get straight to it. I'm ready to do this so I'm going to do it.
>
> T: I'm sorry. That isn't how I work. We did discuss this on the phone. And, to be honest, I don't think it would be the best for

you, even though I understand that you feel some pressure to tell
me.

G: [appears not to have heard me and launches into his story] I was
sexually abused when I was a kid and . . .

T: [interrupting] Okay, stop, Greg.

G: . . . it was just horrible . . .

T: [interrupting] Greg.

G: . . . Those assholes . . .

T: [interrupting] Greg. [louder] Greg.

G: What?

T: I don't want you to talk about it yet. You are getting more agi-
tated as you talk about it. Can you feel that?

G: I'm there. It's happening. I can see . . .

T: [interrupting] Stop, Greg.

G: Why would he do that?

*As mentioned before, just about every trauma therapist encoun-
ters this kind of situation. The new client is determined to spill
his trauma story, becoming more and more dysregulated and dissociated. I know I must stop him, but he is not easy to stop. I will
endeavor to get his exteroceptive senses engaged so he can see where
he is right now.*

T: [interrupting] Greg.

G: [seemingly to the perpetrator] Why would you do something like
that?

T: Greg!

G: What?

T: [pointing to the painting on the wall] Tell me what colors are in
this painting here.

G: It's full of red.

T: What other colors are there?

G: Green, yellow, white, blue, pink.

T: Excellent, excellent.

G: Pink, green.

T: And what color is the wall?

G: A creamy color.

T: Good. So tell me where are you right now, *actually?*

When a client is immersed in flashback, the question "Where are you?" can be tricky. If the therapist is not careful, the client will answer from the flashback, "I'm in the forest surrounded by the gang," or some such. I am being specific by emphasizing where he is now. That usually helps the client to focus on now.

G: In [names our city] in your office.

T: That's right. You were getting quite upset, weren't you?

G: Yes. I want to talk about sexual abuse. . . .

T: [interrupting] No, not yet.

G: [interrupting] I'm upset about it. . . .

T: Of course.

G: . . . I can feel it happening in my body right now. I can feel him
    . . .

T: [interrupting] I want to tell you something you don't know.

G: He's touching me. . . .

T: [interrupting] Stop, Greg!

G: What?

T: Can I tell you something you don't know?

G: I know that that's happening.

T: It's *not* happening is what I want to tell you. It's a memory.

A flashback is a very intense memory (Rothschild, 2000). Grasping this concept is integral to recovering from traumatic stress. The client must, eventually, realize that the intrusive images and flashbacks are all actually forms of memory, no matter how real they feel. And activating exteroceptive senses is a major way to help make this distinction. Exteroceptors link an individual to now even while the flashback is pulling his awareness into then.

G: I can see it.

T: It's a memory you're seeing. Where are you *right now?*

G: I'm in your office.

T: That's right. Tell me something you see *in my office.*

G: I see a carpet.

T: Yes, what color?

G: It's red.

T: Good. What color are the shoes you are wearing today?

G: Tan.

T: What size are those shoes?

G: Eleven and a half.

T: What size shoes were you wearing back then? Were they size 11s?

G: [chuckles a little] No. I was only 8, they were like size 6 or something. . . . Oh no! I can see him about to touch me. . . .

T: [interrupting] Wait a minute, stop, stop, stop.

The questions about the color and size of his shoes now were helpful. But when I asked him what size they were in his memory, he slipped back into the flashback; so that question was not helpful. I will not ask that again, at least for now.

G: . . . I can smell him . . .

T: [interrupting, louder] Greg!

G: What?

T: What color is the rug here?

G: Red.

T: Have you ever been to Disney World or Disneyland?

I'm switching topic right now for several reasons. For one, it will draw him away from the flashback. In addition, there is an important principle that I believe I can teach him if we get the right resource. I'm picking the place on a guess. If it doesn't work, I'll ask him to choose something. But luckily, in this case it does work.

G: [looking rather surprised at the change of topic] I have, Disneyland.

T: What's your favorite ride?

G: The one where you fly over California.

T: Soarin' Over California?

G: Yes.

T: That's my favorite too! Can you remember it right now?

G: I can.

T: Can you remember it really intensely?

G: Yes, especially the lemon smells from the citrus groves.

T: And do you remember when you lift up your feet because you're going over the trees? [We both lift our feet, remembering.]

G: Yes.

T: Are you on that ride now?

G: No.

T: I'm glad you know that. But it's a really intense memory, right?

G: Yes, it's awesome! I love it. I've been a couple of times.

T: Terrific. And you know that this is a memory even though it's intense—the smell of the lemon trees, the feeling of the soaring—it is not happening now. You know that is a memory?

G: Yes. I'm remembering it.

T: A really good memory.

G: Yes it is.

T: So here's what I want you to know: It's the same when you feel like the bad stuff that happened before is happening now. That's a memory too.

G: It feels more real.

T: I understand.

G: It hurts. . . .

T: I understand that. You're *remembering* how much it hurt, and emotionally you can still feel the pain of it. *And* it's not happening, *it's a memory.*

G: [slipping back into the flashback] He's drunk. . . . He's coming towards me. . . .

T: Greg!

G: Why are you shouting?

Sometimes it is necessary to shout to get the attention of someone during a flashback. Flashbacks tend to be very loud and often the person cannot hear the therapist. It is important that when the therapist needs to be louder than the flashback that he is not shouting in anger. There is a big difference between just loud and angry loud.

T: I was stopping you from going back into it. Sometimes it is hard for you to hear me, so I need to be loud. Where are you *right now*?

G: In your office.

T: And the rug?

G: With the red rug and a pretty painting. Lots of colors on the painting.

T: So tell me, do you feel better when you know you're in this room, looking at that funky painting, or when you're off remembering that other stuff?

G: Oh, much better in this room. The other, it's horrible! I think about what . . .

T: Did you know you could stop it?

G: Seems like you stop it for me.

T: I interrupt, but you stop. You respond to my stopping you. That's a big step towards you becoming able to stop it on your own.

G: Oh, okay.

T: Look at your shoes. What size are they?

G: Eleven and a half.

T: And what colors on the painting?

G: Yellow, orange, brown, gray, red.

T: I want you to be able to stop it yourself, in here *and* on your own, before you talk about it more, because that's the way for you to do it safely and to be able heal from it.

G: Why? I thought I should just talk about it.

T: Not when you are so out of control of it.

G: What if this is the only session we have, then I would never talk about it?

T: I want you to leave here feeling better than when you came.

G: That would be awesome.

T: And it's my professional opinion, only an opinion—mind you, I could be wrong—but it's my professional opinion that you will feel better and more steady leaving here if we stop you from going into that.

I do believe in my disclaimer, also in regard to my work with clients. I could be wrong. Bottom line: I have to work in a way I believe is safe. Not to do so would compromise my personal and professional integrity. My preference is to work in partnership with the client, so if he will let me, I want to explain to him how I came to my point of view. That will give him some added information on which to base his own opinions and ultimately his decisions about how to proceed.

G: But it feels like I must tell you . . .

T: Let me tell you a couple stories about me. Would that be okay?

G: Yes, that's nice because it's not just me telling things.

T: So in the old days when I didn't have very much experience, when I was a new therapist, new to the job, I did like you want now and just let the new client tell their trauma stories first thing. And when they would do that I had many occasions where clients would be afraid to come back. Some just felt so much worse they didn't dare continue. Others told me that I knew too many of their secrets, all those bad things that happened to them. As a result, I became like the representative of those bad memories. You see, we didn't know each other yet; they had nothing else to link me to. So after this happened a lot of times, I started thinking maybe it wasn't the best idea to let my new client tell all. That if the client tells all those horrible things before we develop any kind of relationship, maybe that's too scary for them. That's why I am stopping you: I want to make sure you're feeling safe enough to come back. Does that make any sense to you?

G: Yes, that helps.

T: That was one story. Can I tell you another?

G: Okay.

T: Most of my clients and I have found that being able to *control and stop* those memories that intrude into their minds, and into their bodies, can turn out to be more important than telling the story. But that does *not* mean they can't ever tell it. Once they have that control, some decide they do still want to tell their story. At that point it can be a good thing because they've got the good self-control, mind control, body control, that help them manage the telling without it making them come unglued. That's what I would prefer for you. But you need to think about if that would be right for you.

G: I think I understand.

T: What do you remember about what I said?

G: That when you were a new therapist, your clients would just jump into stories about abuse and stuff and tell them over and over again, but you found that people became unglued. Then it sounds like you figured out some ways that made it better to talk about things. You also said that people maybe don't want to come back if they feel like everything's been given to you before they know you, then they feel too vulnerable or ashamed. I get that.

T: So that's why I'm stopping you even though I understand you came with a different expectation. I'm not meaning to disappoint you, but I'm meaning to stop you from coming unglued.

G: But I still think it would be good to tell a story so it's not in my head anymore.

T: I agree it would be good not to have it in your head anymore. But I'm not convinced that telling the story would be the way to do that, at least right now. Have you told the story before?

G: Yes. To some other therapists and in AA [Alcoholics Anonymous].

T: Did those tellings get it out of your head?

G: I guess not if it's still there. . . . Oh no! It's happening, I can see it. . . .

This is typical. Greg does grasp my logic, but is still pulled into the flashback. I'm not worried as this is just a first session. I think it is encouraging that he responds so well to my stopping him and that my reasoning appears to make sense to him. We may repeat this scenario many more times before he can take control himself.

T: Greg. Open your eyes, Greg. Greg, Greg, stop.

G: What?

T: Who am I?

G: Babette.

T: What color is this rug?

G: Red.

T: And where are you *right now*?

G: In your office.

T: With what size shoes?

G: Eleven and a half.

T: Good. I'm being strict about this, as you can see.

Again, part of the partnership, to own up to my strict limits. He continues to respond well.

G: You are a strict teacher. You are really strict. But I feel better seeing the rug than the abuse.

T: Could you imagine why I need to be strict about stopping you?

G: Can you tell me?

T: Because right now you can't stop yourself.

G: It controls me?

T: Correct. And that's the thing with those kind of memories, they feel like they control you.

G: Well they are.

T: I'm quite confident that I can help you turn it around so that you can control the memory yourself.

G: That would be good.

T: It takes a little time and some effort, but it doesn't take forever. And it's much easier if you don't talk about it than if you do.

G: Well, I would rather not be upset. I think you used the word *unglued*. I don't want to be unglued. That's not a nice feeling. Because when I feel unglued, that picture comes into my head and . . . oh, I see it happening again. . . .

T: Stop! That's me being strict.

G: Yes. You stopped me.

That was quicker! Progress.

T: Soon you need to make a decision about whether that makes sense to you as a way to help you. If it doesn't, then it would be better to find you a different therapist, because I can't work that other way anymore.

This is a very legitimate option for him. Certainly I can find a therapist who would let him tell his story unfettered. I hold to my belief that the client knows himself best, so the decision must be his.

G: I know I feel better right now when we're talking right this minute, but I don't know if it will really help.

T: I understand. You might investigate this yourself: If you make another appointment, you can make an experiment between now and the next time. When you get caught by the memory, make yourself look at your shoes and really see what size they are now. Look around the place you are actually in and describe a few things you see. And keep reminding yourself that the pictures in your mind's eye are memories. Could you do that?

I'm encouraging him to take charge of the self-control. Experimenting is a very good way to try something out without committing to it.

G: Yes, I think I could. That sounds like a good plan.
 T: Then when you come next time, you'll have a stronger basis for
   deciding how you want to proceed.
G: Yes. Thank you.

Greg did return for the next session and engaged in a course of therapy geared to improve his self-control and stabilization. Once he decided that was the way to go, he progressed quickly. Within a few months he was well in control of his flashbacks and in a good position for Phase 2 memory processing.

As Promised

At the beginning of this chapter I proposed five major advantages of applying principles from the sensory nervous system to trauma therapy. The annotated transcript, above, demonstrated how drawing on extero-ceptors can quickly anchor a client, even a brand-new one, in the present moment. Below I will expand on these others that are also so useful in helping clients to safely work in both Phase 1 and Phase 2:

- *Phase I: quickly and reliably stabilize dysregulated states of anxiety, dissociation, panic*

As demonstrated with Greg in the above session transcript, shifting a client's attention to utilizing his exteroceptive senses ("what color is the painting?") quickly steadies his state of arousal and his emotion.

- *Phase I: efficiently stop flashbacks*

There are detailed discussions for stopping flashbacks in both *The Body Remembers* (2000) and *8 Keys to Safe Trauma Recovery* (2010). The central principles involve identifying a flashback as a memory (which it is) and then accessing exteroceptors to underscore that the trauma is not happening in the present moment. Though I did not use an entire flash- back procedure with the new client, Greg, in the above session transcript, I did introduce those principles to stabilize him during the session.

- *Phase 1: Consistently distinguish past from present including differen- tiating a reaction to a trauma trigger from the original traumatizing event.*

It is very common for an individual suffering from PTSD to confuse a reaction to a trauma trigger (fear, hyperarousal, racing pulse, and so on) with a possible repetition or reemergence of the earlier traumatic incident. This is understandable as the nervous system may react to the trigger in the same way it did during the original event. The most helpful tactic in such an instance is similar to the intervention for a flashback discussed above: First, identify the intense reaction as the result of a triggered *memory* and use exteroceptors to anchor the client's awareness in the present moment.

- *Phase 2: Confidently maintain awareness of the present moment while simultaneously remembering what happened in the past.*

This is a fairly simple and straightforward process that involves shifting between exteroceptors and memory, that is, paying attention to what is seen, heard, and so on in the present moment, and the traumatic mem- ory. These principles will be further explored and applied in the Chapter 8 discussion of mindfulness.

- *Phase 2: Increasingly identify and implement current and past resources to antidote the terror of past trauma.*

Applying this idea to the client in the above transcript, Greg, in a future session, we will use his memory of Soarin' Over California, his favorite

ride at Disneyland, and other pleasant memories to antidote his memory of abuse. That will be enabled through having him notice how he
feels *now* when he remembers the good memory and encourage him to
experience it. This strategy is similar to the way in which some methods of trauma therapy process trauma memory, taking a piece of the
memory and noticing the effect in the body (interoceptive, somatic, and
autonomic aspects of the nervous system) and emotions in the present
moment. Shuttling back and forth between the current effect of the aver-
sive memory and the current effect of the positive memory will assist
resolution of the traumatic memory. Levine (2010) would call this *pendulation*. Such an intervention is not the entirety of a Phase 2 therapy,
but can serve as a useful adjunct to any method (prolonged exposure, Eye
Movement Desensitization and Reprocessing, Somatic Experiencing,
and so on) to increase the safety of the processing as well as the success
of any therapy. Identification, development, and application of antidoting
good memories will be expanded on in Chapter 6.

Summing Up

Some years ago, after showing another video demonstration during a
large professional lecture, a man in the audience raised an objection to
my application of dual awareness by directing the client in the film to pay
attention to her exteroceptors. Among other things, she had identified
my hair color and the type of earrings I was wearing. "You call that 'dual
awareness'?" he said demeaningly. "Why, that's just simple distraction!"
Though I didn't take his bait, the question got me thinking. Here was a
therapist who had learned a technique called "distraction." How sad, I
thought, that he acquired an intervention that he could imitate without
any understanding of why it works, how to use it, and what it does. In
such an instance he has no chance of bettering that technique or further-
ing its development because it is just that, a technique, with no theory
or principles to build on or utilize to adapt it to the needs of a particular
client.

Please note that these strategies are but a few of those that can be created from a thorough understanding of the sensory nervous system. I encourage you to take the theory and principles from here and reform them with your own clients on an individual basis. Consider what is happening with the client in the moment and how awakening her sensory connections could help. This will open a mass of possibilities for stabilizing your clients.

CHAPTER FOUR

Revitalizing a Lost Art

Trauma Treatment Planning

If you're trying to create a company, it's like baking a cake.
You have to have all the ingredients in the right proportion.

—Elon Musk

History taking and treatment planning seem to be lost arts, particularly in trauma therapy. Nowadays many therapists falter under pressures that professionals did not know in the 1970s. Most clinics and third-party insurance payers drastically limit the number of allowable sessions. If you only are permitted five sessions, dare you use one (or more) of them for history taking and goal setting? And all too often traumatized clients enter the therapy room for the first time filled with enormous pressure (or expectation) to spill the story of their traumatic experiences into the room. Do you let them? Do you stop them? In addition, I often hear trauma therapists assert that history taking is unnecessary or burdensome in light of the fact that they know they will be working on trauma anyway. Moreover, many adhere to trauma therapy protocols that do not include history taking or assessment. All of these circumstances can make treatment planning difficult. The result may compromise client safety and possibly the entire course of the therapy.

A Historical Perspective

On my first postgraduation job as a clinical social worker for Jewish Family Services in St. Louis, Missouri, in the mid-1970s, treatment planning was a central focus of supervision sessions. All first client sessions focused on history taking and assessment, *not* treatment. I was required to record the client's current living situation, significant developmental issues, work history, physical and mental health history, use of drugs and alcohol (past and present), and encounters with violence and other adversity ("trauma" was not yet in our vocabulary) and discuss at length why the client was coming for therapy and what had precipitated the decision to call for that first appointment. My supervisor and I would then discuss each new client, evaluating his or her history, reason for coming to therapy, strengths and weaknesses, and defense mechanisms. She would pull out her 136-page copy of the second edition of the *Diagnostic and Statistical Manual of Mental Disorders* (*DSM-II*; American Psychiatric Association, 1968) (by comparison, the current *DSM-5* has 991 pages!) and we would discuss and then determine a diagnosis. Next we would proceed to speculate on plans for the client's treatment that centered on the client's stated long- and short-term goals for coming to therapy—what he wanted to accomplish immediately and in the long run. Those plans would then be confirmed with the client. In subsequent supervision sessions we would review the initial goals and plans in the light of what was actually happening in the therapy and adjust the treatment plan accordingly.

That was just about 40 years ago and I do not remember most of the clients I had during that time, except for one who particularly stands out because she had trauma-related issues and the weirdest diagnosis I have ever encountered. She was a young woman with what we might now identify as issues rooted in early attachment and trauma caused by neglect and physical abuse by her (then) teenaged parents. In her early 20s at the time I saw her, she was still living with, and rather dependent on, her hippie father. Her reasons for coming to therapy were to get along better with her father and to be able to find and keep a job. My supervisor found the most appropriate diagnosis of the time, Inadequate Personality, 301.82 in the *DSM-II* (American Psychiatric Association, 1968, p. 44)—a diagnosis which no longer exists. And then my supervisor asked me, "What are her defense mechanisms?" I thought for a moment and then astounded both of us by replying, "Well, actually I think much of her problem is that she doesn't really have any!" Surprisingly, when we referred back to the *DSM-II*, we found that my evaluation actually fit well with the diagnosis of Inadequate Personality:

> *This behavior pattern is characterized by ineffectual responses to emotional, social, intellectual and physical demands. While the patient seems neither physically nor mentally deficient, he does manifest inadaptability, ineptness, poor judgment, social instability, and lack of physical and emotional stamina. (p. 44)*

Based on this, we agreed that in order to help the client to reach her goals, the treatment plan needed to include (contrary to what one might usually think) *developing and increasing* her ability to defend herself. In essence, I would be helping her to develop defense mechanisms and make them effective. I remember one of the first things the client and I agreed to do was to teach her how to *not* answer a question. Her lack of defenses left her vulnerable to giving up any and all information about herself at the slightest invitation. She was a much too "open book."

At any rate, the required careful evaluation and treatment planning was a highly structured approach to doing therapy. I, along with many of my colleagues—most of them recent graduates like me—would groan as we complained about our supervisors' assignments and the amount of paperwork that was required. Nonetheless, those labors and that structure provided a secure framework for my work that served me well then and has continued to serve me throughout my clinical career. I cannot even begin to imagine how I would have figured out that early client and effectively helped her toward her goals without it! The value of a careful and comprehensive history, discussion of client goals, and development of a treatment plan cannot be underestimated.

The Value of History Taking

Would you want to be thought of by your own therapist as "the rape case" or "the tsunami survivor"? When you skip history taking, you lose out on getting a three-dimensional picture of your clients. They might, then, remain in your mind in a single dimension, that of their traumatic experience or experiences. I have always preferred the 3-D view. It is way too easy to make crucial errors because critical information is missing. Moreover, history taking should not just be about collecting information on adversity. That well-spent time forms the beginnings of the therapeutic relationship. It is also an opportunity to gain perspective on the client's talents and resources, which can be central to a successful trauma therapy. There will be a lengthy discussion of resources in Chapter 5, but for now suffice it to say that if you do not familiarize yourself with your client's resources—past and present—you are missing very important parts of the overall picture.

As mentioned above, a thorough client history should include:

- The client's current living situation
- Current network (family, friends, religious, social)
- Family of origin structure and function
- Significant developmental issues
- Current occupation and work history *or* current school grade and student functioning
- Physical and mental health history including diseases and hospitalizations
- Past and present use of alcohol and drugs (legal and illegal)
- Trauma history, *titles only, no details* (see below)

Some therapists obtain this information through an interview; others have clients answer questions on a form. There are pros and cons to both. My preference is to do this in contact with clients. In that way I can also monitor how they react to the various points and help to keep their report emotionally manageable (per Chapter 2, by observing and regulating the ANS).

Tracking the client's state while taking history is particularly important when asking about adversity and trauma. There are at least three critical considerations for keeping the history taking within manageable bounds. The first is to take it slow so you can track and modulate client arousal. Second, keep the report of these events to titles only; the more details, the greater the risk of decompensation or dissociation. The third is to put an emphasis on resources, especially when asking about trauma.

It is very important that the report of trauma history should be limited to titles *without* details. Just saying "I was raped," or "I survived a tsunami," and so on can be extremely challenging for some clients. Adding details would provoke most into highly dysregulated, and possibly dissociated, territory. Once a trauma experience has been named, following that up by asking clients how they have coped in light of that event will extract resources that can both help to modulate the history taking and, if noted for later use, will aid regulation during the therapy itself, whether it is Phase 1 or Phase 2. Examples of questions that will flesh out the client's history with adversity include:[*]

- Have you experienced accidents or falls?
- Have you experienced any form of violence—sexual or physical?
- Have you been diagnosed and/or treated for life-threatening illness?
- Have you been hospitalized for mental or physical illness?
- Have you had surgery?
- Have you experienced a natural disaster or terror incident?
- Have you witnessed violence or a serious accident of another?

---

[*] Many trauma professionals like to use the Adverse Childhood Events questions from the Felitti et al. (1998) study. If edited, they may be useful in gathering important information. However, as written, I (as well as my clients) have found them much too detailed, provocative, and triggering. If one of the goals is to maintain a safe and contained history taking, that much detail, I believe, is neither necessary nor advisable.

- Have you suddenly or traumatically lost a close friend or family member?
- What was a typical type of childhood punishment?
- Any other incidents of risk to your or another's life or bodily integrity?

The suggestions in both of the lists above are guidelines and are not meant to cover every eventual important question. Make sure to consider additional ones that are relevant to a particular client or your specific point of view.

Compassionately Contain Intake and Assessment

At the same time that trauma therapy should be a partnership with decisions mutually agreed upon, there are definitely times when the therapist must assume the role of director. This is particularly necessary with clients who need help to regulate states of arousal before they are able to do this for themselves. When safety is an issue, the therapist is obliged to step in and put on the brakes (Rothschild, 2000). Taking a protective, directive role can be very consistent with a client-centered partnership, particularly when the purpose is made explicit and agreed to by the client. Often, however, stepping in with directions may be necessary even in an initial session when dysregulation or worse is a risk factor. As demonstrated in the session with Greg in the previous chapter, for the new client, being interrupted, slowed down, or even stopped can be disconcerting even when it is protective.

While I clearly advocate for history taking, including obtaining a list of the general types of traumatic experiences a client has endured, I do not want clients to recount, narrate, or detail their experiences unless and until they are stable and can digest and integrate what has happened to them (Janet's Phase 1). Often, as in the session with Greg, it is necessary to dissuade a new or continuing client from impulsively recounting their experiences. This area is probably the most controversial among the topics that I teach and nearly always elicits similar questions: "How can I prioritize stabilization when my new (or continuing) client insists on telling me the details of their traumatic incident or history?" That common question bears witness to how difficult it can be for therapists to stop their clients, even when the therapist knows that further destabilization is a risk. I must, however, argue that trauma professionals are obligated to stop clients from spilling their stories into therapy rooms (and over the phone) before a therapeutic contract has been established, and, more importantly, when clients are not able to constructively manage the telling. If allowed to go forward, clients will routinely dissociate, go numb, become anxious or panicked, freeze, and so on. This is *not* a kindness nor is it helpful. It *is* a kindness, however, to stop clients, protecting them from this kind of risk—even when interrupting feels or is perceived as rude. I think about it like this: It is also kind to protect young children by taking matches away even when it upsets or feels rude to them.

So how do you do it, that is, interrupt clients who are absorbed in the telling of their traumatic experience? Really, it is not hard. You can simply say, "Please stop for a moment." If a client does not hear you, has become or is becoming immersed in a flashback, you may need to raise your voice (flashbacks can be loud). Maybe you will have to repeat yourself or just say, "Stop!" Once you have the client's attention, it is helpful to explain why you interrupted. I will tell my client that I can see increasing distress and am becoming concerned. Then I usually ask, When you have told this part of your history to others,

- Has it helped or hurt you?
- Do you generally feel more solid or more unglued from the telling?
- And so on.

Those who have been in the habit of disclosing their traumatic experiences in detail will usually recognize that the result is not pleasant, even if they feel some kind of release in the short term. More likely they routinely become dissociated or panicked. Making that explicit can help to dissuade a client from continuing. Admittedly, it can be more difficult with the person who has never told anyone what happened and is hoping to finally have that opportunity. In these and other similar circumstances

I routinely reassure clients of at least two things. For one, when they are stable enough to manage the telling, I will be there to listen. And for the other, just knowing the title of what happened (per assessment guidelines, above) gives me a good idea of what happened, even though I do not know the details. Then I reassure them that I want them to postpone the telling for when it will be digestible and help them, not destabilize or hurt them.*

In Chapter 18, "Learning From Mistakes and Failure," in *The Body Remembers CASEBOOK* (Rothschild, 2003, pp. 201–210), I recount a particular instance where I went against my better judgment and allowed a client to go forward with her detailed trauma narrative before I believed she was ready to do so. Long story short, it was a disaster and the client never (so far as I know to this day) recovered from the consequences. I still regret not listening to my own knowledge and wisdom, and have not repeated the same mistake. That has meant, however, that once in a while a client will choose another therapist who is more willing to take the chance. This is okay with me as, at the end of the day, I have to live with myself and my decisions. I would much rather err on the side of safety, even when that risks my client's frustration or anger. It helps me that I am confident that once clients are stable and otherwise well equipped, the telling and integrating of their trauma history can be done in a safe and productive manner.

What Are We Going to Make?

The title of this section, "What Are We Going to Make?," has become my slogan for treatment planning and goal setting. There are also applications of this concept for supervision and even in the corporate world (where some of my students have taken it). The concept developed gradually over several years in my work through my trainings and lectures. And it led to the creation of my very favorite training exercise, which I invite you to try out now. The exercise involves the analogy of baking. I admit

---

* Where disclosure is necessary to protect minor children or others who may be at risk, make sure to follow the rules of your licensing body and laws of your state or country.

that in many ways it is a silly little exercise, but it has—what I believe to be, and my students tell me is—a very useful objective. I offer it to you here to try yourself or with one or more colleagues. It is preferable that you carry out the exercise before reading the explanation which follows immediately after.

Baking Exercise

Read these two lists. List #1 includes these ingredients:

- Eggs
- Milk
- Butter
- Sugar
- Flour

List #2 consists of these foods:

- Cookies (some of you may call them "biscuits")
- Cake
- Bread
- Pancakes (some of you may call them "crepes")
- Scones

The task, then, is to reflect on how you would make the foods in List #2 from the ingredients in List #1 with consideration of the following points:

1. Knowledge and recipe required to make it
2. Quantity of each ingredient that is needed
3. Which additional ingredients might be added
4. Order the ingredients must be mixed (matters for some, but not all, recipes)
5. Choice of equipment
6. The temperature required for cooking or baking
7. Total amount of time needed to create the finished product

Exercise Explanation

Most bakers realize that to achieve a successful outcome, they need to know what the end product is supposed to be prior to beginning the process. What is involved in making chocolate chip cookies is quite different than baking bread. Of course, once in a while someone can be very lucky baking haphazardly. However, planning a little ahead by making sure that you have the ingredients, that you know how much time the item takes to make from start to finish, that you have the equipment and ingredients that you need, that the oven or stove you are using can reach and hold the necessary temperature, and that you have the right recipe will all go a long way toward ensuring a successful—and edible—result.

Not so oddly, the same principles apply to all types of psychotherapy and particularly trauma therapy. Planning ahead, including being clear about what you and your client are aiming to accomplish (what you are going to make together), and confirming that you have enough time and the right tools or techniques at your disposal will go a long way to ensure success in therapy.

Now you might think that this sounds very common sense (which I agree) and even wonder why I am spending time on this. However, strange as it might sound to some of you, innumerable colleagues, students, and lecture attendees have alerted me that a good deal of trauma therapy is *not* usually conducted in this way. Unfortunately, such lack of planning may be responsible for a lot of therapeutic mishaps. First of all, as demonstrated in the previous chapter, many clients dive into their traumatic stories immediately upon arrival. In addition, I know from questions during trainings and lectures as well as consultation and supervision that many trauma therapists are *not* clear about their clients' short-term or long-term goals. Routinely I ask, "What did the client tell you she was coming to therapy for, what she wanted help with or to accomplish?" All too often therapists either reply that they do not know or remember, or may say something like, "Well, I think he wanted . . . ," which is not at all the same as *knowing* what the client wants.

So why is this important? Is it not the therapist who should be making the decision about what to do in the therapy? I know that many will believe that to be true. However, I would like to argue for a different point of view. In my experience, the most successful therapies are *partnerships*. That means that the client and the therapist decide together the direction and procedure of the therapy. Of course the client will want to make use of the therapist's professional expertise, but that is not the same as wanting (or needing) the therapist to take control of what the client should do. When paying attention to what the client wants to make, both short and long term, the therapist can then evaluate if she is in agreement and if she has the know-how, tools, and time to be able make that with the client. If the answer is yes, then they can proceed. If not, then negotiation or even a referral to another professional might be in order. And, as a matter of fact, research shows that when trauma clients are given a choice for their own treatment options, the treatment becomes more cost effective. (Le, Doctor, Zoellner, & Feeny, 2014). Moreover, a therapist should never be reluctant or afraid to refer a client to a colleague who is better equipped to address that client's needs. It is a huge kindness to do so.

However, that does not mean that the therapist just agrees to what the client wants. A main responsibility of the professional is to see to the client's safety. For example, when what the client wants to make will increase dysregulation or dissociation, then there is an obligation to stop him. As I mentioned previously, not to do so could result in disaster.

Applications of the principles of "what do you want to make" should now be fairly clear for the therapeutic setting. In addition, I would like to give an example of the relevance in a different context, a telephone crisis line. Crisis line counselors often receive calls from distressed individuals who immediately and persistently launch into the telling of a trauma history, often in great detail. That commonly creates a challenge for the counselor: what to do with the story and the dysregulation that regularly results. Often these are one-off calls, but sometimes distressed callers retell scenarios repeatedly to whomever they can. Rather than just listening to the story, it might be more helpful to stop the caller and to ask, "What do you hope to gain from telling me about that?" It might be just to tell another human. But it could have a different motivation. When they do ask, counselors often find that a caller actually wants, for instance, just to feel better, calmer, or have the noise or pictures in their mind go away. Consider this: When something like that is the case, compulsive retelling of the trauma story might make (cause) something quite different than what the caller actually is hoping for. Finding out what callers really want to achieve increases the chances they will get it. At the least it might be worthwhile to attempt something different. The counselor could suggest, "I might be able to help you feel calmer if you *don't* tell me your story right now. Would it be okay for me to try?" If the reply is affirmative, the phone counselor could instruct the caller in grounding, mindfulness, exteroceptive stabilization (per the previous chapter) and so on. The point is that such interventions would directly target what the caller wants and may teach him a strategy he can use again. Likewise, in the therapy setting, checking what the client wants to make at the beginning of therapy and at regular intervals throughout the course of therapy will help ensure that the therapy will be successful.

The principle of "what do you want to make" has relevance in at least two direct ways for professional (and student) supervision. First, I always begin a supervision or consultation session by asking the therapist what he wants to make during the time we are talking, and then also specifically with regard to the client questions that are raised. That way I know what help is needed and can assist in keeping the consultation on track. This is also a principle I apply when juggling questions during professional trainings. Before I am given a wealth of background information, I ask for the point the therapist is aiming for, what she wants to make from her question. That way, when she proceeds to tell me pertinent information, I am in a better position to organize it. This might be an idiosyncrasy of my thinking style, but I find that knowing what the person wants to make orients my mind in a way that (usually) helps my answers to be more on target and briefer. Last, I am often asked questions that fall into the category of, "What would you do with a client who . . . ?" You can fill in the blank with just about anything. Before I am able to answer these types of questions, I ask several in return: "It depends on what you and your client have agreed to make. Are you working in Phase 1 or Phase 2? Have you considered the client's strengths and weaknesses?" And so on. The point is that there are usually many possible directions. The correct (or most helpful) answer will depend on the goal that is at hand and consideration of factors such as the current contract, client resources, the time available, and so on—generally, the factors for consideration that were outlined in the baking exercise above.

Why Now?

Once you know what the client wants to make, a second follow-up question is vital: "Why are you coming for therapy *now*?" This might seem strange to ask of a client who seems clear that he is coming because of this or that trauma in his history. However, the question of "why now?" can reveal additional, critical information. There is nearly always a precipitating factor that determines when a client initiates therapeutic intervention. Often, what in fact precipitates that first call has little or nothing to do with the stated reason. An example might be the client who says, "I am here because I was abused as a child. I want to resolve that." While that may be true, since the issue she wants to resolve happened a long time ago, and the client has been living with that for a long time, it is important to know what made the difference to seek help now instead of at an earlier time or a later date. The question is, "Why are you coming now? What motivated you to make that call?" Take careful note of what the answer is to that question. It may tell you what is really hurting the client right now. The answer may surprise you. It might be that the dog recently died, or a relationship broke up, a problem in the workplace, and so on. So why is that relevant if the client wants help for being abused as a child? Essentially, it makes *all the difference*. In such an instance it is actually the more current event, the one that precipitated the call, that needs first attention. To put off or ignore that and prioritize the stated reason, for example, the early abuse, could put the client in danger of decompensation or worse. It is always the most recent injury that needs the first aid. Think of it as similar to a hospital emergency room triage: What's bleeding? Let the scars wait for attention after first taking care of the injury that is bleeding.

Linda: Why Now? Mother or Work Issue?

This is the initial session with a new client, Linda. As I had informed her on the phone when we made this appointment, on arrival she first filled out a basic intake form that included basic personal history, and then we spent the first half of the time on fleshing that out so I could have a fairly good 3-D sense of her. Once that was accomplished, we were able to go on to discussing her goals—what she wanted to make—with the aim of establishing a therapeutic contract.

My first consideration for this session was to get and keep her ANS calm enough that she could think straight. The second was to clarify what she wanted to achieve in spite of her husband pushing her to therapy. The principles involved in using somatic resources for stabilization here will be discussed in the next chapter. The successful application of those resources in helping Linda stay calm enough to think straight made it possible for us to zero in on the "why now?" that actually needs to be the first focus of the therapy.

> Therapist [T]: Okay, Linda, how can I help? Tell me why you're here.
> Linda [L]: Well, things have really been hard in the last while. My husband said, "You can't keep avoiding this; you have to deal with the problems with your mother." It's as simple as that.
> T: Do you agree? What would *you* like me to help you with?

Any time a client states another's agenda, I must check if she shares that or not. It would never be a good idea to collude with the other's agenda in lieu of forming a solid partnership with the client based on what she wants and needs.

> L: I don't know 'cause I'm not thinking straight.
> T: You're not thinking straight? That's important! Would it be okay

if I helped you to think a little straighter *first* before I asked that question again?

The dysregulation must be managed before we can clarify any contract.

L: Yes, that's okay. I just want to make sure I deal with the problem; he said I really need to talk about it.

T: I understand. But first, can you feel the seat of that chair you're sitting in? Can you feel it under you?

L: [feels chair with hand] Yes.

T: I see you checked it with your hand. I'm wondering if you can feel it under your legs and your bum there?

L: Ah, yes, I can.

T: That's good. Is it hard or soft?

L: Hard.

T: Is that comfortable or uncomfortable for you?

L: It's okay.

You may have noticed that I have not asked this client about her body yet. That is because I don't know her and am not sure yet if a body focus is something she can manage. By asking about the chair, I am encouraging an indirect body awareness, something I call backdoor body awareness, which calls upon the exteroceptive sensation of touch (as discussed in the previous chapter), rather than interoceptive sensations that can, for some, be more activating.

T: I'll be honest with you—I actually prefer the chairs for me and my clients to not be completely comfortable.

L: Why is that?

T: Because when someone sinks into a comfortable chair, her muscles relax, and then sometimes it's even harder to feel calm or think straight when talking about difficult things. So I actually prefer a chair where you and I sort of have to work to sit in it, use our muscles. Helps my client to think more straight and

me to stay more alert. I don't know if that makes any sense to
you.

L: It does a bit. I wouldn't want to sink into a comfy chair right
now. I might get lost.

*To be honest, I don't know if the chair discussion is clinically useful
for Linda or not. However, we are just getting to know each other and
I want her to be exposed to how I think.*

T: As we talk about the chair, do you feel any difference in your
thinking right now compared to when you came in? Are you
more clear or less clear or the same?

*Always a good idea to give a range of possibility instead of asking, "Is
that better?" or some such.*

L: It's going up and down.

T: Anything in particular you notice makes it go up or down? If you
don't that's fine. I'm just curious.

L: Feeling the chair helps some, but my head's still racing. I want
to get on to do what I came here to do. That's what I'm thinking.

T: And that is to talk about your mother, correct?

L: Yes.

T: Before you do, let's check if you are ready to manage that. It
would not be a good idea to dive in unless you are feeling solid
enough to do so. Without going into your mother yet, based on
how you are feeling right now, would your thinking get more
clear or less clear talking about her?

L: I think I'd get more nervous.

T: When you get more nervous, do you think you are more clear or
less clear?

L: Less.

T: I'm glad you know that, because that makes me think that it
might be good to wait a little longer, see if we can help you

get less nervous so you can think straight first. Would that be okay?

L: I understand what you mean, but I am afraid to go home if I don't talk about her.

T: Because of your husband?

L: Yes, he'll be asking me.

T: Since we still have plenty of time left, would it be okay if we did one more thing to help you be less nervous and think more clearly before turning to your mother?

L: Okay, if you think there is enough time. . . .

T: I can see you are doing something with your feet. Are you aware of it?

L: Yes.

T: It looks like they are rocking. Can you show me what to do?

L: Like this.

Sometimes I want to copy a client's movement to see what it feels like myself. Usually such repetitive movements are a kind of self-soothing. And often the client is not aware of either the movement or that it has a comforting quality until I point it out.

T: Is that something that helps your nervousness?

L: It does, actually. I usually exercise a lot. It reminds me of fast walking.

T: Nice! Just so we can see a difference, would it be okay to stop the movement in your feet and the rocking and see how it affects that feeling of nervousness or clear thinking? Then I would want you to do it again and check if there is a difference. Would that be okay?

L: I'll try. [stops movement for some seconds then starts again]

T: What did you notice?

L: It does help to rock my feet. But when I try to stop, I don't completely stop. I can still feel the moving inside.

T: Is that good or not?

L: I'm less nervous. This is good.

T: Oh! So it helps you to make that movement with your feet. And it also helps when you stop because you can still feel it inside?

L: Yes.

T: That's so cool. Now you have a choice: you can continue it outside or inside, however you want. Do you remember ever doing that in a situation with somebody that's uncomfortable? Having a conflict or something?

L: Probably. But I never noticed it before.

T: I think it's something that really helps you.

L: It does.

T: I actually love it that you can take it inside, so that you can feel the movement inside without it being visible outside. Like a secret weapon.

L: It's good. I never realized I could.

T: I think it's a gift you've always had and just didn't know it.

L: Probably, probably, yes.

Anytime a client can become aware of something that soothes and calms is terrific. And if she can do it on the sly, so that no one can see it, that's a bonus. Helping someone become aware of and claim such a resource and then put it to effective use is one of the most rewarding parts of my work!

T: How's your thinking right now?

L: A lot clearer.

She is ready to talk about the issue with her mother, so long as I keep monitoring and modulating her distress level.

T: In that case, we could talk a little about how I could help with your mother. But I want to keep it contained. To start, could you condense into one or two sentences?

L: I can do it in one word: Cruel.

T: And what happens to your thinking and the nervousness when you tell me that?

L: I feel sad, 'cause she tries to help me now, but I just keep remembering . . .

T: When she was cruel?

L: Yes. She tries to help me now, but I just don't want it.

T: She's different now?

L: Yes.

T: I thought that was very cool you could condense it into one word. How's your nervousness level right now?

L: A little bit higher.

T: Go ahead and let your feet move. Can you feel them? Can you feel the movement?

L: Yes, it's good, better.

Both condensing what she had to tell me and checking back in with her feet are helping to keep this first session contained. Remember, we don't even have a contract yet, so letting her tell more could be very unwise and uncontrollable.

T: So you didn't go into detail, but you told me the headline.

L: That was good, actually. I think that says it all. She's so nice now or she's trying to be nice and it's very hard.

T: Like she is two different mothers?

L: Yes.

T: Let me ask you another question, because we're still getting to know each other, and find a basis for what we might do together. This is what I understand from what you've told me: you're having some emotional difficulties and your husband said that the only way you're going to be able to deal with those is if you talk about your mother. Is that right?

L: Yes, that's correct.

T: Here's my question: *Why now?* From what you say, it's been difficult with your mother for a long time. Maybe your whole life.

But I suspect there's something that made it come to a head, made a difference, so that your husband said, "Now! You can't avoid this anymore. You have to go talk to somebody." What made that difference?

As discussed above, this is a vitally important question. Usually the answer contains the real reason someone comes to therapy and illuminates what she actually needs help with.

L: I'm struggling in a new job, still on probation. I have a difficult boss. Everyone else is leaving the place because of that boss, but I really want to do this job.

T: Are you telling me that the added stress of the job has made it that much more difficult to deal with your mother?

L: Yes.

T: Okay. That's important. There are actually two issues here: There's the historical issue with your mother that is continuing to impact you, and then there's this current issue with your new job and boss. They may or may not be related, but it sounds like the job issue is more pressing and has a more immediate, critical impact. Is that correct?

L: Oh yes. I need this job!

T: Then I am wondering, would it be a good idea to look at the job and boss issue first?

L: Yes. It's very needed.

T: That makes sense to you?

L: Yes. But I'll need some courage. The job needs to be sorted out. A couple of days I've been too upset to go in and that could get me fired.

T: Okay, I think that's a good idea to work on the job issue first. We may find there's a relationship to your mother and we may not. So shall we focus on the job first?

L: Yes.

We now have a contract. Further work is required to decide how we are going to work on that, but the contract is clear. This session provides a good example of the reason that digging for the answer to "why now" is so important. If I had just gone with the initially stated goal of dealing with her mother, the result could have been disastrous. That would have been a mistake for several reasons. First, it would have been following her husband's, rather than her own, agenda. In that way, she (and indirectly, I) would have been responsible to him; he would have, figuratively, been in the room directing the therapy. It is never a good idea to follow a third party's agenda. Second, I wanted to find some way to reduce her nervousness and help her to think more clearly. Not much could be accomplished in the dysregulated state she was in at the start of our discussion.

There was so much trauma and confusion tied to issues with the mother that going along with that as the first therapy goal rather than the job issue would have been a big mistake. The ensuing destabilization caused by opening that Pandora's box would have made it more difficult, possibly impossible, for Linda to deal with her difficulties at work. Actually, it could even have worsened the work situation because her, admittedly, clouded thinking would have hampered her competence and also ability to separate the boss from her mother. There is no doubt that Linda faces challenges with her mother, but those will be much easier to deal with once her job situation is stabilized.

Later in the therapy, Linda confided that she had been very relieved at that first session that I did not go into her mother "stuff"; she actually had hoped I wouldn't. At the same time she acknowledged that the work issue was, indeed, the bigger problem at the time, but that it was harder to talk about because it was "so immediate."

Spaghetti vs. Salad

It is a common occurrence in trauma therapy for the client to come in wanting to make something that conflicts, or is not consistent, with what the therapist wants to make. Often this happens when the client goal or the precipitating factor is something recent and the therapist believes it is better or prefers to target earlier issues. Some of you may be thinking, "Am I not the professional who knows what should be worked on first or at all?" Those of you who do, consider a different point of view: The clients are the ones who have to live with the results. The therapy should be about their life quality and emotional health. Here is an analogy: How would you feel if you went to a restaurant and ordered spaghetti, but the waiter brought salad because he thought that would be better for you? Might you feel mistreated or diminished in some way? Just like in a restaurant, the client should be able to order what she wants. Then, of course, it is the therapist's judgment and choice if he will make that with the client or not. For one thing, the therapist must consider if what the client wants to do is safe at that point in time. Possibly what the client wants to make needs to be postponed until stabilization is secured. In that case, negotiation with the client is the first task.

On a personal note, I have experienced a therapist changing the tack of what I wanted. A couple of decades ago, I suffered a particularly distressing loss. Maybe someday I will write about the details, but for now suffice it to say that I was bereft in a way I had never known in my life to that point. Though I had good support from my network, several friend-colleagues encouraged me to engage a therapist to help me over some particularly difficult humps. At the time I was already a very experienced therapist and supervisor in my own right, and it took me some time to shop for a professional who would not be intimidated by my experience, and with whom I would feel comfortable to be candid and emotional. After phone calls to a dozen or more highly recommended professionals, I settled on three to meet with in person. Each, in their own way, interviewed me about the current situation and also asked about my history. The first therapist kept commanding me to make eye contact every time my gaze averted so I could think or take a break. Her constant demands to "look at me!" had me fleeing her office with relief. The third, a psychologist, turned out to be the winner. She was kind and competent, with good boundaries and plenty of old-school wisdom. However, it was my experience with the second one, a body psychotherapist, that is relevant for the discussion here. I was familiar with him from my professional network so felt more quickly at ease. I was clear with him that I was seeking help for a recent bereavement and was open to history taking because I agreed that the 3-D perspective (as discussed above) is useful to have. Nevertheless, something went wrong. In discussing my current loss, I exclaimed something like, "I've never been so sad in my life!" This prompted him to ask if I had experienced any other significant losses. I had and mentioned a particularly difficult early loss, when I was around 3 years old. For some reason, unknown to me then or now, he latched onto that earlier loss and, forgetting about the recent one, took me down a road to explore my feelings about that early experience. In that situation I was very much a vulnerable client and not identified with or connected to my competent therapist self. So I followed him down that road, discussing the impact of that earlier loss. *Both of us* forgot about the current one that had brought me to him in the first place, and I became disjointed, discombobulated, and disconnected. By the time I left his office I was in a daze. Later that evening and into the next day I felt very anxious, sometimes on the verge of panic. It wasn't until the following evening, while having dinner with a friend, that I realized what was going on with me and why I felt so unsettled, split, and destabilized. That therapist had diverted me from my bleeding wound by focusing in on an old scar. Oh my gosh, that was horribly disconcerting and ungluing! Once I grasped what had happened and was able to reconnect with my current grief, I calmed down. Though I returned to feeling very sad, I was no longer anxious and disconnected. However, I was angry. I had been very clear in stating what I wanted to make, and that therapist had prioritized another agenda. In doing so he misguided me away from my current hurt into the past. Needless to say, I did not return to that therapist and continued on with the psychologist I mentioned above.

As unpleasant as that experience was, in a way I am glad it happened. It drove home the ramifications of (returning to my analogy) being served a salad when I had clearly placed an order for spaghetti. Though I had seen, heard about, and speculated about such consequences previously, I had never met that experience personally. This was an enlightening, if disruptive, lesson that strengthened my teaching and clarified my supervision in this area.

Think about this for yourself: How many times has a client come in with a current issue that you believed had roots in earlier distress or trauma? Do you usually lead a client to work with the earlier issues instead of the more recent ones? Do not be surprised if you do; this happens all the time. I have certainly done it, particularly before my own distressing experience. Consider the result of such a practice. Is it then easy to resolve the earlier issue? From what I have observed personally and professionally, it is *much* more difficult to resolve those early issues when they are targeted *in lieu of* a more recent one. The emergency room analogy from the "Why Now" section above applies here too. If the client comes in telling the therapist what is bleeding, but the therapist is more interested in old scars, the client can, figuratively, bleed to death—that is, become weaker, less resilient, decompensated. I have seen this happen too many times. I have personally experienced it. When that happens, the fix is for the therapist to let go of that current therapeutic direction and revisit what the person came in with. Stabilization is nearly always facilitated by doing this. And, of course, this mishap can be avoided by addressing the precipitating hurt in the first place. Remember: When a current issue triggers a past trauma, you do not need to go to the past trauma to resolve the recent problem. That is not avoidance; it is good common sense and may prevent further destabilization.

A final note on this topic: It is a good idea for each therapist to know her own limitations so that she does not agree to therapy tasks that are outside of her range of comfort or skill, or that she believes could be unsafe. When I was living and working in Denmark I received a call from a man who wanted help to contain sexual impulsivity, which was threatening his marriage. But he was concerned how he might feel if, while discussing these issues, he needed to release sexual arousal. He asked if he could do that in my bathroom. At that time my therapy room was separated from my bathroom by only one door, no hallway between. So what he wanted to make did not work for me as my workplace did not provide enough boundary. I asked among my colleagues and found a referral, also a woman, who had a much different workplace setup, with a bathroom far down the hall. She felt comfortable to take on that client; her limitations were quite different. So the client was able to make what he wanted, but had to do it with a different therapist whose workplace could comfortably accommodate his special needs and boundaries.

Keeping the Contract: Una

I had been seeing Una for just a few weeks when she came for the session transcribed and annotated below. The first visit was history taking and goal setting. She came initially because she had read in a popular magazine about the effects of trauma. She had been assaulted and molested as a teen, and wondered if that was why she had never remarried after the death of her husband several years before. Her answer to the question of "Why now?" was that she was nearing the anniversary time of his death and she feared the predictable malaise that she knew would again come over her soon. Using the concept of psychological triage discussed above, it appeared obvious that the wound from her loss was still "bleeding." She agreed, though she felt anxious to consider facing her grief. We first worked with Phase 1 stabilization, which was accomplished fairly quickly. The session, below, marked the start of Phase 2, focusing attention on her loss and on her impending anniversary grief reaction. I am including this session here because it underscores the importance of attending to what the client wants to make and what is "bleeding" now, staying on track despite diversions. Throughout this session, additional principles are demonstrated, including the advantage of mindful body awareness in facilitating integration of the work at hand (no pun intended), and the value of taking smaller steps (to be discussed in Chapter 7).

> T: How can I help you today?
> U: I feel so constricted in here. [points to her chest]

T: In your chest?

U: Yes. As I told you, this time of year it comes over me.

T: This time of year? The anniversary of your husband's death?

U: [nods, then shakes her head] I haven't accepted it.

T: What does it feel like in your chest?

U: It's very heavy. I have to bear it there.

T: What do you bear there?

U: A very heavy thing. I don't know what it is. It hurts me.

T: Physically hurts or emotionally hurts or both?

U: Both. It feels like I can't get enough air. It's very narrow there. I used to go out quite a lot. I feel better when I go out, but as soon as I'm inside it comes over me again.

T: All the time or only this time of year?

U: Mostly this time of year.

T: How long from start to when it goes away?

U: Around the first day of autumn I know it will come soon. He died in November. It gets very difficult when our old couple friends are doing things together and I am alone.

I realize I am still unclear what she wants to make today. So I ask again. . . .

T: How are you hoping I can help you with this?

U: [she still has her closed hand covering her heart area] I'm hoping you can help take this away [rather quickly she casts her hand from her chest, out to the side, opening her hand as if throwing something out of her chest].

Now this is a very clear expression of what Una wants to make: She is saying and showing that she wants me to help her take away the distress she feels in her chest. This will be important for me to remember so I can keep track and steer her back to exactly there when she gets too far adrift from it.

T: Take it away like that? [I mimic the motion.] What happens when you do that?

U: It feels like a release. [She slumps her shoulders and tears come into her eyes.]

T: Something is happening in your eyes. What changes there when you do that, when you make that gesture and feel the release?

U: It feels easier.

T: It looks like your eyes are watering. Is that true?

Though it's likely her tears have to do with sadness, I never want to assume what watery eyes could mean. Humans tear up when they are happy, sad, aggrieved, angry, touched, afraid, in pain, relieved, and so on. It is always better to ask than assume or tell the client what she is feeling.

U: I can't understand why it should be like that for so many years. Nobody can understand. There's nobody I can talk to this way. That's why I came to you, for help with this.

Though I asked about her tears, she evades that question by shifting to a related, but different topic. This is usual in therapeutic interaction, that answers are not always in response to the question that is asked. It is useful to notice when this happens as it usually indicates an area that is difficult for the client. Then the therapist can decide if it is better to back off for a while, or to return to the original question and confront the difficulty. I decide, for now, to let her avoid the emotion, but explore her body sensations a bit more.

T: I notice you are exhaling a lot. Tell me what it feels like in your eyes and throat when you make that gesture.

U: [does it again in the same way] It gets easier, but I feel weaker.

T: You feel weaker?

U: Yes, like I lose strength in my body.

T: Let me understand. You say when you make that movement with your arm and hand, you feel a release but at the same time you get weaker.

U: I lose some strength in my legs and in my body.

T: Hmm. Try doing the opposite motion, whatever that is.

U: [moves her clasped hand back to her chest] It's better, stronger, in my legs.

T: It's interesting. Try that opposite motion again and see if it has a meaning for you.

In Chapter 1, I discussed the importance of meaning and changing meaning for healing trauma. That may be centrally important here if she is to change her relationship to her grief.

U: Yes, when I do that it feels like I take my husband back again. I don't want to throw him away.

T: What happens in your body when you make the gesture to "take him back" and you connect those words?

U: It's like usual. Tense. Aching, especially in my neck.

T: Wow, that's really a huge difference in the effect between the one motion—throwing away—and the other motion—taking him back.

U: [she swallows hard] It's confusing.

It is important for me to remember that getting the distress out of her chest was what she said, and showed me, that she wanted to make this day. It appears that this motion and its opposite have huge meaning for her. I believe it is important to stay with this and will attempt to keep her focused.

T: Try repeating the first movement and the words that go with it.

U: [gestures] I throw him away.

T: You throw your husband away with that gesture?

U: It seems so. And I felt that distinctly when I did it and felt weak.

T: Try also with the opposite movement.

U: [makes opposite gesture] I took my husband back again.

T: How is that?

U: The same as before. I feel more tense and stronger.

T: When you throw him away you feel some release, but you feel weak, particularly in the legs?

U: That's correct.

T: When you take him back, you feel strong again, but more tense, particularly in your neck?

U: Yes, I've held him for so many years in my body.

T: How long were you married?

U: Fifteen years, since I was 19.

T: Of course you hold him in your body. That's a long time to be married to somebody. You slept in the same bed and had sex, affection, and fights . . . all of those things.

U: I still miss him, but I don't want to have pain for him in here. It's an unfair situation. All of my friends still have their husbands and wives. I'm the only one in our network who lost their spouse. It's just not fair!

T: I agree with you that it's not fair. What does it feel like in your body when you say that it's not fair? Say it again and see what it feels like.

U: It's not fair! I get angry. I want to hit the ones who took him away from me. The hospital and doctors and all.

Here is a decision point. It would be easy to go down the anger road with her. And in many respects that would not be wrong. For sure she has plenty of anger over the situation of losing her husband, and also the fact of it. However, expressing anger is not what she said she wanted to make today. She was clear in both words and gesture that she wanted to take away (or at least reduce) the pain in her chest. Therefore, I feel it most wise to gently lead her back to that.

T: Over the last 12 or more years, since your husband became ill and since he died, would you say that you have been more angry or more sad or more aggrieved?

U: I haven't really felt much of anything, not emotionally anyway. Work has kept me preoccupied.

T: So you haven't expressed those feelings you have inside? You haven't grieved?

U: Only a little at this time of year, when I can be alone. I keep it to myself. In the beginning, of course, I talked to other people. I talked to my family. But now I can't do that. They are tired of it and think I should be over it.

Another temptation for direction. I make a note about this, but I'm going to stay with what she wanted to make.

T: These movements that you made [I mimic each]. They seem like very strong gestures. Rather severe. Throwing your husband away and then grabbing him back.

U: Hmm.

T: Are you agreeing with me?

U: [nods]

T: Part of grief is letting go of someone, but not necessarily throwing them away. When I say those words, do they make any sense to you?

U: Yes, but I don't know how to do it.

Here is where both sticking to the task of what she wanted to make and also making use of her good body awareness and apt gestures might come together—as long as I go gently.

T: I would like to suggest, just as an experiment, that you put your hand back on your chest, the position that feels like you are holding onto your husband. Then try to find a movement that might express something in between holding on and letting go, like a first step toward saying goodbye.

U: [Very slowly she moves her hand from her chest out to the side, gradually opening her hand in a letting-go gesture. She begins to cry softly. I wait several minutes until she quiets.]

T: I see and hear your strong emotion. Can you feel it?

U: Yes. [Another minute goes by.] What should I do now?

T: What would you like to do? [I see her arm begin to move back toward her chest.] Would you like to take him back a little bit?

U: Yes. [She slowly brings her hand back to her chest. Then she raises both hands to her face and cries a bit more.]

T: [I wait, then ask] Do you have words going on in your head?

U: Yes.

T: Can you say them out loud?

U: I must learn to take smaller steps.

Here is a significant change in the meaning of her situation. Rather than pushing herself to do something she feels unready for or holding on in a way that keeps her in pain, she realizes she might be able to let go if she does it slowly.

T: Hmm. Nice. Stay with your feelings and those words for a little while.

U: [breathing easier, calming]

T: How do you feel in your body right now? Do you feel weak or strong or something in between?

U: Relieved. Okay.

T: How do your legs feel?

U: They feel normal, not particularly weak or strong, just like usual.

T: Do you want to try that slow motion again?

U: No. That's enough for now.

I am delighted she knows and can assert her limits!

T: I agree with you. I think taking much smaller steps is a good idea. Like today, the in-between steps, so you are not severely throwing him away or severely grabbing him. You can do this bit by bit, slowly letting go and then bringing him back a little. Sort of like in waves, like a pulsation.

U: Yes, I like that. [She tries the slow back-and-forth movement a few times.]

T: Find your own rhythm. I will be happy to help you with it. Also, if you feel comfortable, you can experiment a little on your own, maybe at night before you go to sleep. How are you doing right now?

U: Well. Peaceful.

T: Is this a good place to stop?

U: I think so.

The result of this session, that Una was able to connect with her grief in a way she had not done before, was a huge step toward her healing from this traumatic loss. Moreover, she realized herself that it would be better to take smaller steps. That is a significant and valuable insight. If I had not kept her on the track toward what she came in wanting to make, none of those outcomes would have been possible.

It is important to remember that trauma treatment must be about the client, her body, her mind, her life. Therefore, always finding out why the client has come for therapy, as well as the motivation or precipitating circumstances, will help to ensure that the therapist meets the client where she is.

PART II

Practice: Applying Theory and Principles

CHAPTER FIVE

Simple Resources Modulate and Even Heal Trauma

The grand essentials to happiness in this life are
something to do, something to love, and something to hope for.
—George Washington Burnap (1848)

H ere is a most humbling statistic:
There are exactly 168 hours in a week.

Why do I find this fact humbling? On average, how many hours per week do you usually see your clients? One hour per week is typical. *One hour!* Within that single hour, just how much support can any therapist provide each client? And then what do clients do for support and to augment their therapy in the other 167 hours per week? That statistic alone tells me that no therapist, *no one*, no matter how skilled, compassionate, supportive, generous, kind, and so on, can be enough for any one client. However, every client must have additional support to be able to recover from trauma. Where might that additional support come from? Many of your clients will already have a treasure trove (tapped and untapped) of additional support available. You (and they) just need to know where to look for it and how to identify and utilize it. Other clients will need help in developing additional options for support. Both of those situations are where *resources* come in, *all sorts* of resources.

Merriam-Webster's 11th Collegiate Dictionary defines a *resource* as (among other things):

- A source or supply of support
- A natural feature or phenomenon that enhances the quality of human life
- A possibility of relief or recovery
- An ability to meet and handle a situation

In *The Body Remembers*, Volume 1 (Rothschild, 2000), I introduced the basics of resources and their relevance for putting on the brakes in trauma treatment. The discussion and session transcript that follows here is meant to augment and update those earlier ideas and applications.

One of the greatest pleasures of my writing and teaching is to be able to identify and adapt theory and interventions that I learned in my early psychotherapy education in the 1970s and 1980s—long before I ever heard of the conditions now known as trauma and PTSD—and apply them to the trauma work that I teach and write about now. It feels like mining, polishing, and then sharing gems that have been buried in the past. That is really a parallel process to the topic of this chapter, as that is exactly what I am advocating here, to help clients connect with resources from earlier in their lives. In the first three sections I will be resurrecting forgotten resources from the archives of earlier psychotherapy models that can be used toward the recovery from trauma today. The final section of this chapter will feature a depth therapy session transcript that demonstrates how many of these concepts might be assembled and applied to better equip a PTSD client who faces further traumatic challenges.

Wil Baumker's Magic Shop

In the early 1970s, Wil (Wilbert) Baumker, a psychotherapist trained in *transactional analysis* (TA)—popularized by Eric Berne (1964) in his book *Games People Play*—began to do a sort of carnival act at TA conferences (Baumker, 1978). This shtick, as it were, became a very popular (as well as productive) highlight of workshops and conferences for many years. Then, as many shticks do, its popularity faded and Wil gave it up for a more traditional psychotherapy practice. What a shame! The Magic Shop has so much to teach about the resource value of defenses and the care of resources in general.* I have wanted to write about the Magic Shop for a long time—and do talk about it at many of my trainings—as I believe the core principles are brilliant, accessible to all, and, most importantly, have the potential to be very, very healing.

Here is how I first encountered Baumker's Magic Shop.

I was a novice therapist studying TA and Gestalt therapy while working on a master's degree in social work in the mid-1970s. As part of my training, I attended a TA conference and stumbled upon a Magic Shop breakout workshop. Acting like a carnival barker, Baumker was dressed in a flashy jacket with a big bow tie (. . . and maybe a straw hat). I was stunned; did this have anything to do with therapy? But I was intrigued and stayed to watch and listen.

Baumker pitched, "Step right up! Come to my Magic Shop and barter for anything you desire. All you have to do is trade in what you don't want any more." Then someone would approach the booth and say, for example, "I want to be more assertive, to trade for the ability to say 'no.'" And Baumker would then ask what she would exchange for that trait. "I want to stop being a pushover," she might say. Then Baumker would scratch his chin and respond something like, "Hmm, I don't know. . . . Assertiveness and saying 'no' are pretty valuable commodities, two of my best sellers, as a matter of fact. And being a pushover, who'd want that? I wouldn't be able to trade that to anyone. You know, I have to stay in business here. I can't just give away valuable tools and get junk in return. Why should I accept being a pushover in trade? I can't see how being a pushover could possibly be of equal or greater value than saying no. Why would any one want it? . . . Are there any advantages?" That would give the customer pause, and she might reply, "Well, it might keep me from having to make decisions I am afraid to make. . . ." Baumker would encourage, "That's a

---

* The earliest mentions I can find of psychotherapeutic usage of "Magic Shop" are in books on Psychodrama (Schutzenberger, 1965; Petzold, 1971). Whether Baumker was inspired by these or created this version himself is unknown to me.

good start. At least I'm a little more interested. What else does being a pushover do for you?" And so on.

In this way Baumker would prod and encourage the customer to promote and sell the resource value of the defense she wanted to give up, in this case, her defense of being a pushover. Eventually, in essence, the customer would leave the Magic Shop with *both* resources, the one she had wanted to trade in and the one she had wanted to get in exchange. Magic Shop was (and still is by the few who continue to practice it) a genius device for helping people to recognize and value resourceful traits that they have previously regarded as liabilities. Truly, Wil Baumker elevated respect for the resource value of defenses to a literal art form.

You could try this yourself. First think in terms of one of your own defenses that you would rather be free of. Then identify what strategy you would like to replace that defense with. Next, apply Magic Shop principles to recognize the resource in your defense. Write down a list of the advantages of the defense. After that, write down the advantages of the other behavior, the one you wanted to replace your defense with. Are there any similarities on the two lists? Are they complements? What would be the advantages of having both mechanisms in your behavioral repertoire?

Then follow up with this same procedure with one or more clients, targeting a behavior they want to be free of and what they would like to substitute. It is often helpful (and inspiring) to share the story of Baumker's Magic Shop with a client. I have yet to meet one who did not grasp and appreciate the idea, at least in principle.

Natural Resources

We now have so many psychotherapeutic therapies and prescription medications for helping people to recover from trauma that it is easy to forget the wealth of additional potential recovery resources that are at hand within, around, and available to anyone who has suffered trauma. For thousands and thousands of years humans have survived—and even thrived—in the face and aftermath of trauma, long before there was psychoanalysis, psychology, psychotherapy, psychopharmacology, and trauma therapy. It is undeniable that humans are programmed to survive adversity. The very actuality of our continued existence is a testament to this fact. So how did we as a species do it? How have we survived trauma to this point in time? What are the major innate resources that people have used? First of all they have used each other: family, friends, and community (neighbors, religious groups, helping others, and so on). Faith and spiritual belief and pursuits of all kinds sustain and heal many. For example, Alim et al. (2008) found that the most important factor associated with resilience in the wake of trauma was "a sense of a higher purpose in life." And then there is the value of useful work that keeps many a person going. The daily structure and preoccupation of mind can be a helpful counterpoint to the disruption of trauma.

It is disturbing that in the past few decades, reliance on psychotherapy has superseded these tried and truly timeless resources. When did it happen that the therapist became more important than the best friend or that people came to rely more on calming medications than their faith or good work? Do not misunderstand me here. Of course I see value in psychotherapy—I am a psychotherapist and I have had plenty of my own therapy. However, I believe that the equilibrium between therapy and other resources has become imbalanced. What therapists offer clients should be an *adjunct* to a treasure trove of otherwise readily available resources. A major part of the professional's job should be helping clients to identify, access, and develop resources that they can readily make use of in their daily lives, in the 167 hours in the week that they are not in therapy.

Ethan Watters (2010), in his vitally important book *Crazy Like Us*, cautions about the dangers of ignoring natural and innate resources when attempting to help people in different cultures. He studied the effects that globalization of Western psychology has had in other parts of the world.* Contrary to the benefits that were expected, the results were very

---

* Which, by the way, is a an active trend, particularly in the treatment of PTSD (Forbes et al, 2010).

disturbing, particularly with regard to traumatized individuals, families, and communities. Watters found that when a people's traditional ways of handling adversity were set aside in favor of more progressive methods from the West, psychological havoc—not healing—resulted. For comparison, try to imagine, as Watters does, how a trauma clinic in Chicago or London would respond to a group of Aboriginal healers insisting that their native rituals were the only real cure for trauma.

During the time I was living and working in Copenhagen, Denmark (1988–1997), I provided pro bono supervision via e-mail to a Danish psychotherapist who had volunteered with a prominent international helping agency in Sierra Leone during the civil war there. She was running groups, particularly for women who had suffered rape. I wish Watters's research and wisdom had been available to us both at that time. Instead, we were dependent on common sense. Hopefully, I was of help. One of our exchanges is particularly relevant to the discussion here. The young Dane wrote to me in dismay that what she had been taught to do for victims of rape in Scandinavia was not of *any* use to her in Sierra Leone. She was floundering. As she had learned, she tried to teach the women grounding methods and encouraged them to talk about their feelings. However, they resisted, telling her what they wanted to do was "encourage each other to 'get on with it.'" Hers is a good example of the perils of trying to impose treatment methods from one culture onto another culture. My advice at the time (though on reflection, I'd probably advise the same now) was, "This is a situation where it is best for you to learn from them. Ask these women to teach you about how their culture copes with adversity, including rape, and then help them to do that better."

I urge all of you who are working with people of, or in, different cultures to read Watters's book. It will help you to avoid hurting where you are intending to help. And the wisdom of Watters's findings is not just relevant in third world countries. Right here in the West, individuals, families, and communities all have their own survival mechanisms that are vital to recovering from traumatic stress. While it is clear that psychology can play an important role, we who intervene should first be learning about the tools that are already at hand and then helping to maximize their effectiveness. Watters is arguing for a return to the roots of human recovery, similar yet different in every culture. In one it may be a spiritual ritual or religious confession, in another gardening or the laying on of hands. Meditation, talking with a friend, volunteer work, communing in nature—these and many other resources should be remembered, practiced, encouraged, and respected.

Every day, people triumph over trauma through their own natural resources. There are examples of it everywhere, including newspapers and television. Three well-known personalities come to mind: Nelson Mandela, Oprah Winfrey, and Dr. Maya Angelou. All survived horrendous trauma through support of family, faith, and good work. Part of Dr. Angelou's story is particularly relevant and poignant to recount.

Dr. Maya Angelou's Resources

One of the most inspiring public stories of the conquering of adversity through a wealth of resources comes from the autobiography of Dr. Maya Angelou (1969), *I Know Why the Caged Bird Sings*. It is nearly impossible to read this stirring account of her early life without being moved. She suffered terrible early trauma, including rejection by both parents at the age of 3 and rape at the age of 8. She responded to the rape by becoming mute for over 4 years—almost unbelievable for this woman who lived most of her life enriching the world with her words and her voice. The challenge I give to my students when reading or hearing this account is to simultaneously allow themselves to be moved—as one might be by the trauma history of a client—but also to keep enough professional distance that they can pay attention to and make note of *all of the resources* that saved Dr. Angelou. This is similar to what I recommended in Chapter 4 when doing an assessment or taking a trauma history.

When Angelou and her brother (aged just 3 and 5 years old) were forced to travel alone to their grandmother's home in Arkansas, there were innumerable strangers, particularly rail personnel, who saw to their safety, making sure they transferred from one train to the next so that they did, indeed, arrive at their destination. The grandmother took in Angelou and her brother and cared for them lovingly if sternly. And there was a family friend, Mrs. Flowers, who took the young Angelou under her wing and saw to her literary education. Angelou and her brother returned to the care of the grandmother after a brief, if tragic, stay with their mother in Chicago where the rape occurred. It was Angelou's resulting traumatic mutism itself that precipitated the return as the mother could not deal with her mute daughter. And going back to be with her grandmother and Mrs. Flowers was wonderful for the young and traumatized Angelou. Under Mrs. Flowers's guidance she discovered her love of literature and poetry. And eventually it was that love of poetry that helped her to find her voice again. It is through her voice, both written and spoken, that Angelou reinforces the huge value and healing power of resources of all sorts (see another example in the next chapter).

As recommended in Chapter 4, during your next client intakes or assessments, as you are getting the client's history, pause after the mention of each adverse event (if there are more than one, this is particularly important) and ask the client, "How did you survive that ordeal emotionally; how did you cope?" Of course you will acknowledge if the client is still suffering from whatever it was she endured, but the point is to find out what tools and resources she used to survive at the time and continue to employ as she lived with the fact of it since. You may find out, for instance, that a major resource is dissociation or numbing. It could also be that the client relies on his work, spiritual beliefs, nature, a pet, or a friend. Whatever it is, psychological mechanism, belief system, animal, or human, you will be finding out about the client's store of resources. Even if the defense mechanism is not particularly effective anymore, or the closest human or animal ally has died, there are still vital elements of resource to be mined and cultivated. Resources beget resources. Often you only need to identify one and then others become more visible. You will enrich your clients' lives at the same time you ease the therapy. Facing trauma—in the recovery or resolution phase—is always easier when one feels a solid base of resources underneath and around. That goes for the therapist, too: Being in touch with *your own* resources will also help you to modulate the intensity of the difficulties of your work.

Swimming With Dolphins

Asking about resources will help you and your client to begin to grow a toolbox to draw on to put on the brakes, get calm, find relief. However, just as no client reveals all of his history during initial interviews, not all resources will be mentioned, or even suspected, at that time either. Sometimes a resource will emerge spontaneously and unexpectedly.

David Boadella, the father of the European Association for Body Psychotherapy (EABP) and founder and longtime editor of the body psychotherapy journal *Energy and Character*, shared a most poignant discovery of a client's resource during his keynote address at the 2010 EABP Congress in Vienna. He had been working with a very distressed young woman for some time, though their progress was limited due to her fragility. Both were becoming frustrated with the therapy and Boadella was feeling concerned that he could not find any way to help her. Then, during a therapy session many months into their work together, for the first time he became preoccupied by a pendant the woman was wearing around her neck. He realized she wore it often, but he had not really noticed it before. Boadella saw that it was a dolphin and became curious. In his trademark direct manner he asked, "Why are you wearing a dolphin around your neck?" "Because I used to swim with dolphins," she softly replied, looking about rather nervously. To say the least, he was surprised, "Really! What was that like?" With the prompt of that question, the woman calmed a bit as she began to remember and shyly describe the wonders and pleasures of swimming with dolphins. He realized he had struck resource gold and asked what it felt like in her body *now* as she remembered swimming with the dolphins. She was able to identify and feel that her current state had changed from nervous to calm and fragile to solid as her mind and body recalled her experiences. It was the first time either of them had witnessed her become steady and both were encouraged. Her body memory for those experiences was very strong and surprisingly easy to elicit. Remembering the dolphins became the foundation for her therapy, making it possible for her to find—for the first time in years—oases of peace in her tumultuous world.

In Chapter 1, I discussed how important it is to pay attention to the effect a trauma has in the present. That is what needs to be changed in order for someone to recover from or resolve trauma. The same goes for resources. Making use of the current effect the resource evokes will unleash the resource's supportive and healing power. In many cases the current effect of a resource can fully antidote the lingering effects of trauma. (This will be expanded on in the next chapter.)

Everyday Resources: Maryellen

Way too many everyday resources go unnoticed. Many trauma treatment models, including EMDR and Somatic Experiencing, make use of resources such as a *safe place* or *anchor* when working with specific trauma memories. However, resources include much more than those. There are body resources, movement resources, spiritual resources, people, animals, inanimate objects, and so on. And they are useful for anybody at any time, particularly for our clients to help them manage the stresses of their daily lives. Resources are not just for dealing with flashbacks or processing trauma memories, but—and maybe more importantly—for all types of stresses, trauma-related and otherwise. Engaging resources of all sorts improves quality of life. It is easy to forget that a resource can be almost anything. What makes it a resource is that (doing, thinking about, remembering) it helps to calm the autonomic nervous system and gives a feeling of calm, support, or safety. The important thing is to tune up both your and your client's antenna for identifying and capturing resources, including ones that may seem small, minor, or so common that they are easily missed.

In the transcribed therapy session below, I help Maryellen to identify, cultivate, and harvest resources that will help her to face and manage an impending scary medical treatment. The first one that we identify and cultivate is actually a repetitive, habitual behavior. From there her repertoire of resources rapidly expands.

Maryellen

Maryellen has a congenital defect that has required multiple surgeries throughout her life. Most have gone well, but the last one was quite difficult. As a result, she has been suffering symptoms of PTSD, including flashbacks. Further, because of the complications of that last surgery, she will require at least one more. She has become so frightened and hospital-phobic that she panics before or during each medical consultation. At times she has been unable to keep a doctor's appointment because she is so distressed.

The contract is clear: During the assessment Maryellen stated that she sought consultation specifically for help in being able to manage her anxiety. She wanted to be able to get to the hospital for pre-op appointments and manage the surgery itself. At this time she neither wants, is stable enough, nor would the timing be right, to process the memory of the traumatic surgery. She is still in crisis so Phase 2 memory processing would be inappropriate at best. As cultivating resources is useful in any phase of trauma therapy, particularly for Phase 1 stabilization and safety, that is what we agreed to start with in this first therapy session. I was determinedly on the lookout for anything she might do with her body that appeared to soothe her in any way. Additionally, I listened for and asked about any supportive contacts or behavioral strategies she might already (consciously or unconsciously) have in her repertoire. My guiding principle here is to identify existing resources as a path to developing additional ones.

Therapist [T]: How are you today, Maryellen?

Maryellen [M]: [stuttering] Ummm, I don't know how I'm doing. I don't know how I'm doing. It's difficult. [She is sitting tensely, head ducked, eyes darting, holding her hands tightly as she rolls her thumbs over each other.]

At first I am just observing. I want to see how her anxiety is expressed in her body and how she is managing to contain it. Often habitual behaviors have something to do with attempts at calming or soothing. I'm looking for clues. She is somewhat pale and her breathing looks quick. These are indicators that her autonomic nervous system (ANS) is quite activated. I'd say it's in the sympathetic nervous system II (SNS II), orange, area. I note that as a starting point and hope to lower her arousal into SNS I, blue, or even the complete calm of parasympathetic nervous system II (PNS II) green before we end the session. During the session I will keep track of shifts in the ANS as well as following what we are talking about. Changes in the ANS will tell me whether what we are doing is going in a good (calming) direction or not.

T: I see you're holding your hands right now. Can you feel them touching each other?

M: Yes.

T: Are they warm or cool?

M: [softly] Sort of cold.

T: And can you feel your breathing?

M: I can, but it's not very comfortable. I feel a bit like I can't catch my breath.

Cold hands and breathlessness coincide with SNS II. Often, bringing attention to body sensations can be stabilizing. But I am alert in case it is not. If a client has an adverse reaction to feeling her body, other interventions must be used instead. In this case, we are lucky: When Maryellen's attention goes to her hands, I can see that her breathing eases a bit. I am encouraged to take that awareness a step further.

T: I notice your thumbs are moving. Can you feel or see what you are doing with them?

M: Yes, I'm rolling them.

T: When you do that, does it have any effect on you, for better or worse?

M: I do this a lot. Is that okay?

 T: Of course! Does it help you?

M: Yes, I think so.

 T: Can you tell what the effect is when you pay attention to it?

M: [concentrates on her thumbs for a minute or so] I can hear you better and talking is slightly easier.

Talking is easier because, I can see, her breathing has slowed and deepened a little. Moving toward SNS I.

 T: I'd like to try that too. I saw you did it automatically. Would you mind if I copied you? I'd like to see how it feels to me.

M: [hesitantly] Okay.

 T: Help me do this like you. What direction are you going?

M: That way, like that.

 T: Am I doing the same?

M: Yes.

I am aiming for several things here. For one, I really do want to know what it feels like. For another, I want Maryellen to feel some control in the session. And, further, I am hoping that because I am actively doing something with her, she will feel my interest and support.

 T: It's comforting to me when I do that. Is it comforting to you?

M: It is. But I feel a little bit silly.

There is always the danger, when mimicking a client, that she might feel shamed. Obviously that is not at all my intention. So I need to clarify and repair any possible shaming.

 T: Oh, sorry! I didn't mean for you to feel silly. I like how it feels. How about you?

M: Well, yes, it's kind of nice. To be honest, I feel a little better actually.

T: Do you? In what way?

M: I could just feel the panic that keeps coming up . . . but then something changed.

T: When you focus on your thumbs, it changes something?

M: It does actually. I feel more steady. I feel I'm in the room. Ha! I don't know where I was.

T: I'm glad. I focused on it because I saw you doing it. I didn't know if it would be helpful to you. I think I'm going to borrow it from you, when I get in a nervous state, because it feels sort of nice.

M: Really? Now I don't feel so silly if you would use it too.

I really meant what I said. It can be meaningful for some clients to realize that they can teach the therapist something, or that they have a resource the therapist admires. However, something like that can never be forced or phony. This is not a technique, though I will admit I am alert for opportunities to empower clients in this way.

T: When we began, you said your hands were sort of cold. Are they still?

M: Hmmm, now they are getting a little warmer.

That's another indication that the ANS is calming, going toward the blue SNS I.

T: So now I'm curious. Can we experiment with this a little bit?

M: [slightly skeptical] Okay . . .

T: What happens if you move your thumbs in the opposite direction? Does it make any difference? See if it feels any different. Is it more comforting, less comforting, or the same?

The idea here was to explore and possibly expand on this resource. And it doesn't hurt to engage the client's curiosity about the positive effect of what she is doing. Also, giving wide choices (more, less, the same) helps the client to give an accurate appraisal and response. If, instead,

I had her try the movement and then asked, "Is that better?," I would be leading her to an answer I desired. That would make it harder for her to say what was really happening.

M: Probably a little more actually.
 T: Interesting . . .
M: It's more definite.
 T: In what way? Can you tell me what changes in your body? Maybe your heartbeat or breathing?

Body awareness questions are easier to answer if they are specific. And by asking about heart and respiration, I also get a read on her ANS arousal.

M: I think my heart is a little quieter, not so strong in my chest. Breathing is a little easier.

ANS is calming.

 T: That's terrific. I'm wondering, what if you go back the other way?
M: [rolls thumbs in the first direction] It feels lighter. [smiles] I want to laugh when I do it this way. It's more serious when I do it the other way, more solid.
 T: Hmm. That's really fascinating that it's so distinct. I didn't know if there would be any difference, so I'm glad you tried! Actually, I can feel a difference too, so I can follow you. It's different moving in one direction than another. Very cool. So you know it works for you here in this room. Do you think you could remember to try it when you found yourself in a difficult spot somewhere else?

Just practicing in the session is not enough to make it available in the client's daily life. There needs to be a plan to try it out and evaluate it in a stressful situation.

M: I suppose I could. I know I do this anyway when I'm nervous.

T: But do you usually pay attention to it?

M: Not so much. I know I do it and I know it comforts me, but I don't know why I do it; it's automatic. I don't know why it helps.

T: It doesn't matter why as long as it comforts you, helps you feel calmer. It's a little gift.

M: I guess it is. It's nice to have it.

T: So how could you remember to pay attention and also try some variations?

M: Maybe next time I go to an appointment I could have a string or ring around my thumb. That would be unusual and might call my attention to it.

This is what I mean by "cultivating resources." We have identified something the client uses automatically, expanded her awareness of it, and encouraged experimenting with variations. Now it's up to her to put it into conscious practice. I will check with her at the next appointment to see if she remembered and, if so, how it worked. If necessary, we can then make any adjustments for her to further experiment.

T: I'd like to suggest that you also write it down now before you leave here. Write what we've done and what you want to try and how you will remember. Would that be okay? There's paper and pen beside you on the table.

It really helps to have clients write notes to take home. Best for them to write themselves. Increases the chance they will remember under stress. I always keep paper and pen available for this purpose.

M: Yes, okay. Thanks.

T: [after she's written that down] Are you ready to move on to something else?

M: I guess so. Depends on what that would be.

T: I was wondering if you have any other things that comfort you, automatically or purposefully?

I don't want to overload her, but I also want to take advantage of her increased resource awareness. Waking awareness of resources tends to awaken more resources.

M: When it's been tough in the last while—and I know I have a lot of things I have to face, and I'm not sure how to face them— what I do is I go in my bedroom and close my door. Then I put the music up really loud.

T: Nice! Particular music?

M: I like all sorts. But for this I need rock music.

T: Is it the volume or the kind of music?

M: It's both. I get up and dance. I just get up and dance. I shake with the music in a nice way. I dance and I shake my arms.

T: You look a little bit shy to tell me that.

M: It's not like me. I'm normally very quiet mostly. But because I've been struggling sometimes I fly off the handle. Then people tell me to keep quiet. But when I play loud music, they actually don't mind.

T: I'm really glad to hear that. I'm very interested to know the things that you already do that help you. I want to help you with the difficult things too, and it's important not to forget the things that help you when we're focusing on the things that are difficult. Do you know what it is about the music?

M: It's the heavy beat. I like to stamp my feet. It's on carpet so no one really hears me. I take my shoes off, so I can do it as heavy as I want. I feel that my feet are really steady on the ground when I stomp like that. But I can't play loud music and dance at the hospital. . . . I wish I could. . . .

T: I wish you could too. I have an idea, though. I don't know if you can do it, but I have a little challenge for you. Can you sit there quietly right now and remember dancing and stomping your feet? Remember what it's like in your body?

M: Um, yes. . . .

T: And how does it feel when you remember that?

The idea here is to see if we can make this resource portable, something she can use outside of her bedroom. Engaging cognitive and body memory helps. In this way we are cultivating a somatic marker (Damasio, 1994) for the music and dancing.

M: It's good.

T: In what way?

M: I feel I'm doing it. I feel my muscles going even though I'm not really dancing.

That is normal, to feel muscles engage when remembering or anticipating physical movement. The Feldenkrais (1972) method makes use of this phenomenon as part of their somatic therapy, and athletes often practice moves mentally to learn and reinforce them. In this way, the same principle makes it possible for Maryellen to make use of her dancing resource even when she cannot actually dance.

T: I had you try that because I'd like you to be able to have some secret tricks that you can use in public situations. So when you find yourself in a difficult situation or you are waiting—we know you're going to do a lot of waiting—and you can't turn on loud music and get up and stomp your feet, you can call up the mind and body memory of doing that.

M: Maybe I could take my iPhone with songs on it so I could actually hear the music and feel the beat. It feels good. I feel the anger coming out when I do that. It's a nice idea to do it secretly because otherwise people aren't very happy with me.

T: Good point and a good idea! How might you remind yourself if you're sitting in a waiting room or something like that?

It's important to have a plan and try it out when the client is not so stressed—sort of like a fire drill, to prepare for access when stress is high.

M: Maybe put something on my hand or on my bracelet. That's the one place I would look. It might be enough to just make a mark with a pen.

T: You want to try it?

M: Sure. Why not?

T: Here's a pen. Go ahead and try it.

M: [draws a symbol on her hand]

T: What if somebody asks, "What's that?" What are you going to tell them?

M: It's just a reminder for myself.

T: It's private to you. You don't need to say more.

M: That should be good.

T: How are you feeling now? How is your breathing and the temperature of your hands?

M: My hands are pretty warm compared to what they were. And I forgot about my breathing so it must be good.

All good signs that she has become calmer. I believe she is now in the green PNS II range of ANS arousal. This is good; we can keep going. Still, I need to be alert to changes, particularly if her arousal rises again. We are on track with our agreed goals, what we are intending to make, identifying and utilizing tools to help her be more calm.

T: Let's have you write that one down too. [Maryellen writes.] So now you have your thumb rolls, your music, and the stomping and dancing. Are you aware of anything else that helps you?

Now that we've opened the resources box, it is likely that Maryellen will start to think of more things on her own that she might use to help herself. It's kind of like priming the old water pump. You just have to get it going and then it starts to flow on its own.

M: Yes, but I feel a bit embarrassed to tell you.

T: Well, wait a second, then. You actually don't need to tell me. You can if you want, but it's only important that *you* know what it is.

It is important to make sure my client does not reveal more than she is comfortable with. I am also reminding her that she has control here.

M: No, I think I want to tell you. Just so that you don't think I'm silly. . . .

T: What helps one person may not help another. But a resource is a resource. I can't imagine I would find one of your resources silly. But don't feel you have to tell me.

M: No, I want to. When I was young, my mother hung a picture of an angel in my bedroom. I still have it. I used to talk to the angel, tell her all my secrets.

T: Ah . . . I feel very touched when you say that.

M: Because I couldn't tell my family . . .

T: There are many of these kinds of things we don't share with everybody.

M: So that's what I remember.

T: The angel in the picture, what do you call her—is it a her?

M: Yes, a girl angel. I just call her Angel.

T: So Angel is still very alive in you?

M: Oh yes!

T: Where do you feel that or her?

M: In my heart.

T: How do you feel when you remember Angel right now?

M: I feel hugged.

T: Hugged?

M: Like her arms are around me. I don't feel cold or alone. There's a bond, there. I don't need to make any excuses to her. But sometimes it feels a bit silly to talk to a picture.

T: Honestly, I am glad you have had Angel. Do you still have the picture?

M: Yes.

T: Would you want to take it with you? Or would that be too challenging?

M: I'd have to bring a big bag, because it's so big. [shows with hands] But maybe I might take a photo of the picture, on my phone like.

T: There you go. That's smart!

M: To take a photo would be okay. I can still leave the picture at home. Then I would feel more safe.

T: You know a lot of people talk with angels. A lot of people find comfort in that.

M: I haven't ever talked with anyone about it, so I didn't really think about that. But I suppose you are right about that. I don't feel so stupid now. It's nice to think of Angel.

Normalizing is nearly always helpful. First I normalize the resource. Next I normalize her fear.

T: Do you know that most people get nervous about surgery no matter how good their history with medicine and doctors? And that nervousness goes up a lot when things haven't gone well or they have a history of difficult surgeries. Nearly everybody!

M: They really don't in my family. They don't.

T: They don't or they don't tell you? That's two different things.

M: Well, come to think of it, I've seen some look frightened.

T: But they don't talk about it.

M: Nobody says anything.

T: So they might be scared. But they don't . . .

M: They say nothing. They tiptoe around.

T: And that has to make it harder for you because you feel like you can't say anything.

M: That's why I go to my room and I stomp about.

T: Is there anybody in your circle, your network, whom you could tell or have told you're afraid and that it's okay to say, like a friend or more distant relative?

M: I told my niece once.

T: And how did she react?

M: She was lovely. She wasn't afraid.

T: She wasn't afraid that you were afraid?

M: No. She was actually okay.

T: How old is she?

M: She's 16. I was upset and she just asked me what was wrong. It seemed okay for some reason. It doesn't normally feel okay to say, but I said it to her. She was okay with it.

T: I'm glad! Is there anybody else? It's okay if there's not. I'm just sort of exploring with you. A friend or an acquaintance? Maybe somebody at work or in your church?

M: I don't talk to anyone really. I don't get out much because I've been in the hospital a lot.

T: Hmm . . . do you think your niece could accompany you when you go for an appointment or sit with you while you were waiting somewhere?

M: I'd be afraid I'd panic like I did the last few times. I don't want her to see me panicking. She's still very young.

T: Yes, I understand. But there might be something else you can do. . . . Remember what you told me about Angel? How you were going to take Angel with you? Do you think you could do the same for your niece?

M: What do you mean?

T: Take her photo.

M: Oh, I hadn't thought of that. I could do that. That would be good. . . .

T: And maybe tell her what you're doing so she sort of keeps you in her thoughts? She doesn't have to be there with you, but she could hold you in her thoughts and her prayers. Then you'd know someone was thinking about you who wasn't judging you.

M: That would be nice. Sometimes she texts me. I guess I could text her.

T: Then you wouldn't have to worry about if you would frighten her or something like that.

M: It makes sense. It makes sense. I think I'll try that.

We have cultivated many resources today. Now I want to help her make sense of what we have been doing. If she can follow my thinking, she will be in a better position to think of some of these strategies on her own. This is an aspect of Phase 3, integration, using psychoeducation. It is also an important part of creating and nurturing the therapeutic partnership. And last, it goes a ways toward the first goal I mentioned in Chapter 1: to eventually become obsolete.

T: What I'm doing today—I want to make it explicit—you might have already figured it out but I don't want to play a guessing game with you. I was thinking about asking you, "Do you know what I'm doing," but I thought that maybe I'll just tell you: I really want you to have as many resources, tricks, and strategies as possible for helping you to feel more calm, for helping you to feel supported, cared about, not alone. You've come up with several today, and I don't think you have finished with your list. I'm hoping to inspire you to think in these terms more in the next days and weeks and be on the lookout for people who might be able to support you. Maybe check them out a little bit. Also be alert for any other calming or soothing that you notice you do automatically, like your thumb rolling. For instance, watching a particular TV show, eating or drinking something that you hadn't realized was helpful. You might also find you are reading this or that for inspiration—whatever it is.

M: Ha! I know one thing I do and I didn't think about it before: I wear a perfume, and I actually forgot it the last time I was going to the hospital. When I wear the perfume I can't smell the hospital smell.

T: Oh! I like that!

M: I'd forgotten about that. It masks the smell, makes it different.

T: Which perfume do you like to use?

M: Cinnabar.

T: Do you have a little bag that you prepare for yourself when you go?

M: I normally have a bag with me, yes.

T: Maybe you could start putting things in your bag now as you remember them so that when you're more nervous and more under the crunch you'll already have remembered: the pictures, the perfume, anything else.

M: I think that would be good. I didn't realize I had so many options. It's funny—it never dawned on me.

T: Wonderful you remembered the perfume! How are you doing?

M: I'm feeling a lot better. I really am!

T: How long till the next surgery?

M: I don't know. The consultation is in a week and a half's time.

T: You'll find out then? I'm glad we have more time to help you be prepared.

M: Me too. . . . We have at least a couple of weeks. They told me they want me in for some tests . . . so they'll probably want me a week after or so.

T: I'd like you to take your time and settle with this, with what we've talked about today. Think about what you want to put in your bag and pay attention to start doing those things you tried here and notice for better and worse how they affect you through your average day, through the week. Next time I will want to hear about what has gone well and what has not. Then we can see what more will help.

M: Okay.

T: We can't change what's going to happen, but we can totally change the support you feel. We can also change how you manage it all in a different way than you have before. I think we can soften the edges around this difficult challenge you face.

M: I want to get it over with. It's no good putting everything off.

 T: We can keep working in this way until you feel more and more supported and able to manage.

M: Okay. That's better. That's better!

Her color is good and she is breathing easily. She says, "That's better," and I can see that it is! In supporting Maryellen to creatively identify and practice using resources, I have helped her to be less daunted by her impending surgery, once believed impossible to manage. In addition, she is well on the way to recognizing and strengthening her belief in her own innate creativity and resourcefulness.

CHAPTER SIX

Making the Most of Good Memories

Powerful Antidotes to Traumatic Memory

One of the best ways to make yourself happy in the present is to recall happy times from the past.

—Gretchen Rubin

It always concerns me when I hear of trauma treatment that is as (or nearly as) distressing as the traumatic events that bring clients to therapy. Way too many arrive for their first and subsequent sessions terrified in anticipation of what they will be remembering and confronting. I have often wondered: Does it ever need to be that brutal, that hard? As a result, I have been determined to demonstrate that, while difficult, challenging, and at times upsetting, *trauma treatment does not need to be traumatizing*. In addition, I endeavor to conduct my professional trainings in a manner that minimizes risk for traumatization to the participants. Am I always successful? Of course not. But I think it a worthwhile aspiration. One of the ways I approach this goal is by helping both clients and seminar attendees to access and liberally use their exteroceptors, per Chapter 3. When one can easily and quickly anchor in the present moment via exteroceptive senses, stabilization is always at hand. Another useful strategy will be addressed in this chapter, that is the calling up and keeping hold of *good memories* from a person's past. Good memories have the power to stabilize and the power to heal. They, too, should always be at hand.

In thinking about approaching this discussion, I was inspired to look to the arts for reminders of how much humans already know about the power of memories, both bad and good ones. Memories of all sorts frequent the themes of paintings, songs, photographs, and poems. In this moment, several songs come to mind: Elvis Presley's, *Memories,* Jim Croce's, *Photographs and Memories,* and *Try to Remember* from the musical *The Fantasticks.* It has been known through time how such creative records of life can evoke emotion. This chapter will focus on applications of good memories to mediating and healing traumatic memories.

Traumatic vs. Nontraumatic Memories

When working with traumatized individuals on a regular basis it is easy to jump to the conclusion that most all of their memories are adverse ones, or at the least that it is only the difficult memories that should catch the attention of the client and therapist. But that is only a part of the picture and neglects some of the best and most healing aspects of memory. For some reason, it is just too easy to forget that nearly all people—even those with trauma in their backgrounds—have some good memories, often many, in addition to or alongside of their bad ones. Good memories are vitally important, rich with resources that can be cultivated for use in the present. This chapter continues the discussion of resources begun in the last chapter through looking at how past resources are internalized in a person's mental and somatic memory. To help clients in both Phase 1 and Phase 2 trauma treatment, taking note of and paying attention to the pleasant memories as well as the horrific will be vitally important. Memories are linked to the mind and body via *somatic markers* (see below). The somatic markers of good memories are often as (or even more) powerful than those of any traumatic memory. In fact, there are already several trauma treatment methods which, when applied properly, make use of the power of positive memories to mediate the stress of Phase 2 trauma memory resolution work. These include *anchors* (e.g., Somatic Experiencing, Neurolinguistic Programming) and *safe place* (e.g., Eye Movement Desensitization and Reprocessing, Bodynamic Analysis). When properly cultivated in mind and body, good memories can be so powerful that they can *antidote* the undesirable effects of a traumatic memory.

PTSD is hallmarked by intrusive memories of past traumatic incidents. Often those memories take the form of visual pictures or auditory sounds in the mind's eye and mind's ear. It is also usual for these visual and auditory images to be accompanied by somatic symptoms. At times, the somatic symptoms might even appear in the absence of the images, usually as disturbances or discomfort in the interoceptive senses such as increased pulse, dizziness, irritable bowel, and so on. To resolve trauma memories (Phase 2), it is necessary to work with such images and process the associated disruptive and highly unpleasant body sensations and symptoms. How that can be done will be discussed and illustrated below.

Trauma Bested by Resources Past

In 2011, Dr. Maya Angelou was featured in an hour-long interview on a series called *Masterclass* for the then fledgling Oprah Winfrey Network (OWN) cable television channel. Short clips from that series appear on (and disappear from) YouTube periodically. One of my favorite clips is of Angelou telling how she shores herself up prior to curtain calls, lectures, and similar stressful demands in her life, by drawing upon memories of "everyone who has ever been kind" to her. To illustrate the significance of these wonderful memories of all sorts of kind folks—she specifies that they include all races, creeds, and sexual persuasions—she sings a few bars from a 19th-century African American song by Andrew Jenkins: "When it look like the sun wasn't going to shine anymore, / God put a rainbow in the clouds." She then relates how she has had a lot of clouds in her life (see, for example, the story of her early childhood as summarized in the previous chapter), but that she has also had many rainbows. She affirms the advantage of calling up the memory of these rainbows from her life by asserting, "You see, so I don't ever feel I have no help. I've had rainbows in my clouds."

Nearly everyone has rainbows of one sort or another in the clouds of their lives, even amid their traumatic experiences. To be honest, I believe everyone does, but that it may be easy to forget, or even not to recognize the significance of the kindness or support of friends, family, teachers, and even strangers. Years ago, one of my clients told me that one of the most significant people in her highly traumatic young life was a teacher who *once* had said something supportive that acknowledged she could see that something was wrong at home. Even though the teacher had been unable to intervene in my client's traumatic circumstances, the fact that she had seen and said something meant the world to my client. For her it was a sane-making acknowledgment that her home life was not as it should be. She felt seen and cared about, despite the reality that nothing was done about it at that time. The moral of this story is to never doubt the positive impact a kind word or deed, no matter how small, can have for someone.

Another illustrative example comes from my own life. Decades ago I had the occasion to take a young girl under my wing. She came from a very unstable home where periodic violence was the norm. I was able to befriend her and would take her on periodic outings, encouraging her to pursue her love of art and poetry. After a couple of years, circumstances forced us in different directions and we lost contact. Then, amazingly, about 15 years ago, out of the blue, I received an e-mail from her. She had tracked me down on the Internet to tell me that the contact we had those 40 or so years ago had been very meaningful to her, that the memory of my support and belief in her had helped to sustain her through many difficult times.

Memories of all sorts, particularly of people who have been kind, supportive, or helpful, as well as places that have been safe, peaceful, or protected, can be cultivated via somatic and mental memory, and used to assist anyone in their recovery from, or memory resolution of, a traumatic past. One caveat: No resource, human or location, is perfect. Always aim for a *good enough* resource. For example, if Aunt Martha could occasionally be judgmental, call up times when that was not an issue. If the location of the beach resource was sometimes populated by drunken college students, remember it when it was peaceful. If you make sure to help the client to look for a good enough, rather than perfect, resource, just about all of them should be able to identify one or more.

Antidoting Somatic Markers

Somatic markers is the term coined by Antonio Damasio (1994) to describe specific somatic memory. For example, when passing by a bakery a woman smells the fresh-baked cinnamon rolls and immediately her heartbeat calms, her stomach relaxes, and she sighs. A few beats later in her mind's eye she sees her aunt baking in her kitchen and remembers love for and from her. Those physical responses (calmer heartbeat, relaxed stomach, sighing) are all somatic markers for the woman's aunt. Likewise, when a man hears a sonic boom and breaks out in a cold sweat, his heart races, and he can't catch his breath, those somatic symptoms (cold sweat, racing heart, trouble breathing) are likely somatic markers for his combat trauma. Damasio asserts that somatic markers are at play, behind the scenes, usually in the unconscious, as people make all sorts of everyday—as well as serious—decisions, similar to a compass that points them in one direction or another. When somatic markers of adverse experiences are recalled, the tendency is away from whatever is in question; when those from positive experiences are stirred, the tendency is to go toward it.

This is a good place to continue my story, begun in the last section, of the young girl I befriended. When we finally met up again about 40 years had passed. Amazing! The age difference between us did not seem so big anymore, though we still each had feelings for the other from those long-ago times. I still felt and was perceived by her as a mentor or mother figure; she still felt herself to be (and I did too) like a niece or daughter. We had some long talks catching up on those 40 years since we had last met: joys and sorrows, traumas and triumphs. And there were a few things that she told me that were stunning examples of somatic markers. When I had befriended her as a child, I drove a particular automobile. In addition, when we celebrated her birthday,

I took her for lunch and made sure she had a very special dessert. Neither of us ever thought about the significance of either of those details until, when we met again, she told me:

- All of the automobiles she had bought as an adult were the same brand as mine had been at the time I had befriended her.
- When she was stressed at the university and facing exams, she would often buy and eat the same dessert she had enjoyed on that birthday.

Those two facts came as a surprise to me, but made good sense. Both the automobile and the dessert called up good somatic markers for her that were associated with me. Though she may not have thought of me directly, in the background her body was remembering my support and care. Over the years since we had parted, she would access a feeling of support via somatic markers tied to the automobile and the dessert. If she had been my client remembering a supportive person, we could have used those same memories and somatic sensations to antidote the distress of recovering from trauma or processing trauma memories.

Antidoting Traumatic Numbing With Positive Somatic Markers

It is common for repeated trauma freezing to result in a person's shutting off or distancing from emotions of fear and terror. That can also lead to disconnection from any kind of upsetting feelings like anger, grief, and sadness. All defensive strategies enhance coping, though, likewise, they usually exact a cost. In this case, it often happens that in cutting off from the unpleasant feelings, a person may also lose access to pleasant or "positive" emotions such as happiness and excitement, as well as emotions that connect people to each other and are healing such as love, and being touched or moved. Some individuals come to therapy because they feel numb; they have lost touch with their emotions. Often such individuals (and even their therapists) are convinced that the only way to reconnect with their emotions, to enliven the numbing, is through confronting the traumas that have hurt them. It can be extremely difficult to deter these clients, to delay the trauma memory work of Phase 2 until they are stable enough to manage it in a constructive and safe manner. However, if I am going to help clients to wake up their emotions, it is *not* the adverse emotions I want to awaken first. Actually, that idea goes contrary to common sense. A much safer, resourcing tactic is to begin by helping them to rebuild their repertoire of "positive" emotions. Not only will that be an avenue to awakening all of their emotions, but it will do so in a way that they will have a firmer foundation and more tools for eventually managing the difficult, unpleasant emotions when they are ready to face those.

At the same time, while helping a client to reconnect with emotions, regardless if the emotions are pleasant or unpleasant, it is important to never forget that numbing and avoidance are resources just like any other. So pacing the awakening of feelings has to be alternated with remembering how to go numb and how to avoid. Losing access to those resources could be detrimental, even disastrous, for someone who has depended on them for coping with trauma. That doesn't mean they have to continue to rely on those defenses, but that they must be valued and remain in their toolkit for times when they might just come in handy again.

Forgetting good past experiences—positive memories—is a phenomenon that often accompanies the aftermath of trauma, particularly (but not only) among those who react with emotional numbing. This is an area where the understanding of somatic markers can be so helpful. Instead of calling up traumatic somatic markers first, accessing those that are connected to positive events, people, and places is in order.

Enlivening Numbing to Feel Again: Eric

As introduced briefly in Chapter 1, Eric is recently returned from combat military service. He, like many of his comrades in arms, witnessed the injury and death of many of his buddies as well as participated in violent acts himself. Despite a diagnosis of PTSD, he appears to function well at home and at work. However his high-level functioning is deceptive. He reports that he has figured out how to manage his civilian life by cutting off completely from his emotions. In general, he reports feeling emotionally numb. So he functions well, but does not feel that he is really a participant in his life. He has come to therapy hoping to awaken his feelings without having to revisit memories of his war experiences.

Therapist [T]: What do you want to make today?
Eric [E]: I don't want to be numb anymore. I feel dead inside. I want you to help me to feel emotions again.

Eric is clear about what he wants to make. I can agree to his goal, but have one reservation that we need to negotiate before the contract can be acceptable to both of us.

T: I'll be happy to help you with that as long as you agree to not forget how to go numb. . . .
E: What do you mean? That's exactly what I want to stop doing!
T: But there must be some advantage in it; otherwise you wouldn't have developed that capacity. I want to help you to feel more, but not lose the advantage of going numb. Basically to have more, rather than fewer, choices. Does that make sense?

As discussed in the Magic Shop section of the previous chapter, every defense has advantages. Defenses, by definition, are coping strategies. And any coping strategy has times when it could come in handy. The idea is to preserve the defensive option while making it just that, a choice, not an involuntary auto-response, then at the same time to increase the repertoire of alternatives, in this case being able to feel at will.

E: Sort of, but being numb doesn't feel like an advantage. It's like I'm walking dead.
T: I do get that. But think about it—why did you go numb in the first place? Do you remember?

E: Oh yes! It was just all too much. . . . I was afraid I might go crazy from the horror of it all. I felt too angry to function. I nearly hit my wife. That scared me. . . . I don't think I made a conscious decision to stop feeling, but a switch sort of flipped and I was in control of myself.

T: Getting in control of yourself in a situation where you were feeling out of control sounds like a good idea to me. Is that not an advantage?

E: You think so, even though it cost me my feelings?

T: Yes, I think so. You saved your wife from harm and yourself from guilt and possibly jail. And, do I remember correctly: didn't going numb help you to get back to your job?

E: Yeah, all those things. I think I am beginning to understand what you mean by advantage. Being numb keeps my wife safe and me at work. Okay, I guess I see your point. I agree to keep being able to go numb. But I don't really know how I did it.

T: Then maybe that should be the first task for today, learn—or remind yourself—how to go numb.

E: Okay, I agree that's a good idea.

T: Fair enough. We have an agreement for today.

E: So can we work on emotions? [looking askance] I don't remember what it feels like to love my wife. . . .

Today's contract clarified, we are ready to move on to working toward Eric's goal.

T: Something changes in your eyes when you say that. Are you aware of it?

E: Uh-huh. . . . They are a little watery.

T: And do you feel any other changes anywhere in your body?

E: My throat is a little tight.

T: Do you know or remember what emotion those changes, watery eyes and tight throat, might go with?

Numbness is a suppression of feeling, not a loss of emotion. It can feel like a loss because under such circumstances as Eric's, emotion becomes dangerous to feel. The individual wants to cut off the dangerous emotions. But usually they are not that far from the surface. Gently bringing attention to it without needing to make it bigger is like dipping toes in the swimming pool at the shallow end. A controlled taste.

E: Mmmm . . . sadness? A touch of sadness. Maybe I'm not a lost cause.

T: Can you maintain awareness of that "touch of sadness"?

E: I don't know. I'm starting to feel angry.

T: How do you know?

E: My thoughts: I'm angry I can't have my feelings, angry at the war, the government, the enemy that took them away. Oh gosh! I don't want to go home angry. Can you make that stop?

Just a light touch into emotion brings the fear of loss of control. No wonder Eric went numb! Time to remind him that is the resource. . . .

T: I can't, but you can. This is a good place to practice. Make yourself go numb. You do know how.

He visibly works to contain his anger. I see his jaw tighten and his chest constrict.

T: Something changed. I can see you got control of your anger. Tell me what you did.

E: Oh! Okay. I guess I can do that: I tensed up, held my breath, and told myself to stop thinking about it.

T: Good for you! That is so very important that you just did that— both things: that you had a taste of your sadness, felt your anger, and then that you were able to go numb again. That is actually terrific!

E: To be numb again? Really? . . .

T: Let me explain—see if that will help you. When someone has gone numb to block off potentially destructive anger and rage, allowing a softer feeling such as the sadness you just touched into threatens that protective self-control. What you just demonstrated here, even if briefly, is that you are able to visit sadness and still control the anger that you fear will cause you to lose control.

E: I did that? Oh! . . . I did do that! But it wasn't easy. . . .

T: Of course it wasn't easy. You need practice to gain strength and confidence in your ability to contain your anger.

E: That's good to hear. I was afraid I should be all good at it already.

T: Not at all, but you are absolutely going in that direction. A good rule of thumb is to go slowly, a little at a time, to make sure you can stop and contain whichever feelings before opening them up more. That's why I stopped you so quickly, so it didn't build too much. In being able to consciously quiet your anger, you also showed that you can use your body (by tensing and holding your breath) as well as your mind (by stopping the thoughts) to control your emotions. That is fantastic. Those are skills that can be built on.

E: But the amount of anger and sadness was not very much. What if it was bigger?

T: Well, that's the idea, to build the skills in small steps, starting with a little, that will simultaneously build your confidence. It is not a good idea to dive in all at once. I think that was a good-size portion for where you are right now. I don't want us to go any farther or faster than either of us feel comfortable. That means we both can say "stop." Would that be agreeable?

E: Actually, that's a relief. Yes.

Most therapists are trained to allow any and all emotional expression, that catharsis was always a good thing. Here is a clear example of why that is not always the case. Sometimes helping a client to stop feeling, to contain and have control, will be a relief and a safety valve. But it is good to have such an agreement clarified so the client does not interpret that the therapist is afraid of, or indifferent to, his emotions.

T: In that first step you had a taste of memory of your love for your wife, and you felt a bit of sadness that you are not able to feel that love fully now. We can also use other, less powerful positive memories to train up with. Would it be okay to try that?

E: If you think that might help, sure.

T: Is there a memory of a person, place, or activity in your past that you know has positive emotions connected? We could try again with one of those.

E: You don't want me to remember that about my wife?

T: Oh, sorry, I didn't mean that at all. What I meant is that I want you to have a variety of positive emotional memories, some more and some less highly charged.

More options for the client to choose from also means a greater sense of control for him.

E: Okay, that sounds better. I was worried for a moment.

T: I'm glad you asked for clarification! So would that be okay?

E: Yes, I would like to try that.

T: So tell me if you can think of a person, place, or activity that you have known in your past. Something that when you remember it now will have a positive emotional association for you and also help you to feel calmer.

E: How far back can I go?

T: As far as you want.

E: I know what: When I was a kid my best friend Lars and I loved Legos. We could build things with them for hours at a time, day after day.

T: Do you notice any kind of reaction when you are reminded of that?

I am endeavoring to ask the most neutral question I can think of. I don't want to push him toward emotion. He might not notice anything, or if he does it might be a thought, a sensation, as well as an emotion.

E: I know playing Legos together made us happy, but I'm not really feeling anything.

T: That's fine. Good you know that. I'd like to ask some more detailed questions. Okay?

E: Yes, sure.

T: Where would you play with them?

E: In Lars's or my bedroom. Usually on the floor.

T: Do you remember how you would sit?

E: Cross-legged, or sometimes lying on our stomachs. I was often propped on my elbows. I could see a good angle of what I was building from that position.

T: Can you imagine either of those positions in your body right now?

E: Hmmm, yes. . . . I sort of want to get down on the floor. . . .

T: I can't join you because of my knees, but you are welcome to if you want.

E: No, I think I would feel embarrassed. But I like remembering it without doing it.

T: Do you notice anything else?

E: I'm sort of smiling. I'm not feeling a lot, but I'm not feeling quite as numb either. That's weird.

T: Not so weird. . . . This is a very pleasant memory for you, and you can feel that a little in your body. But it is also not highly charged with big feelings, so that lets you edge a bit out of numbness without too much emotion that could threaten your sense of control. At this point, I think it's perfect. A terrific step!

E: That makes sense. But what do I do with it?

Eventually, as Eric gets more familiar and comfortable with sensing changes in his body and emotions, I will be asking more questions about his relationship with Lars and how it feels emotionally and somatically to remember him. I am fairly certain that this old friend is one of Eric's (as Angelou calls it) rainbows in the clouds of his traumatic past. However, before we can take that deeper step, Eric needs more exposure to and confidence at the step we are on. To rush this might risk it backfiring.

T: Well, first, while you are sitting with me, you can practice moving between your memory of you and Lars playing with Legos and your awareness of being in this room now. As you shift between the past and current awareness, notice your body and (to whatever extent you are able) your feelings. Don't push for feeling; just notice if it is there or not. If you find anger building, apply the strategy you used before: tensing, holding your breath, stop thinking about the angry content. Would you like to try that now?

E: Sure. Do you direct me or me direct me?

T: If you want and can, I think it would be good if you try directing yourself. But do narrate when you are switching so I can follow along.

[E does so, back and forth, successfully.]

T: How was that, any hitches?

E: No, it was pretty easy and I only felt a little anger once. But is this going to get me to my emotions?

T: I believe so, though at a slow, safe pace that you can control. Remember, this is only a first step today. Probably practicing at home would be a good idea. What would you like to do for homework?

E: Maybe the same as I just did with you.

T: Sounds good. How often?

E: Once or twice a day. Maybe when I wake up and before I go to sleep.

T: May I add an additional suggestion?

E: Yes, of course. . . .

T: You might also try this when you find yourself in a stressful or uncomfortable situation or mood. Just an experiment to see if remembering playing Legos with Lars can help you regulate other states.

E: Okay, that sounds good.

T: Before you go, please write down what you intend so that you will have the paper to remind you.

Having Eric write down the homework we negotiated will increase the odds that he will actually do it. An outsider looking in might judge this session as very small steps. However, for Eric, it was a huge step to be able to touch on emotion and contain it at the same time. Small, successful steps are always a better choice than bigger steps that risk failure. The advantage of small steps will be expanded on in the next chapter.

There is no reason that emotion must be awakened through suffering. And, in fact, that can often backfire and drive the numbing or dissociation deeper. This session with Eric is an example of a first step toward the goal of reducing numbing, to be able to feel emotions. Subsequent sessions follow the same principles:

- Supporting the numbing as a containment resource
- Small steps
- Pacing each step to his ability and tolerance
- Identifying and using pleasant somatic markers of people, activities, and places from his past
- Agreeing on homework to reinforce and integrate what is learned in the session

As Eric gets more able and confident, past and more current memories with greater emotional charge will be brought in: a teacher, favorite dog, birth of a child, wedding day, and so on. We will continue to swing back and forth between twinges of emotion and numbing, gradually expanding Eric's emotional repertoire while building the ability to both feel *and* contain to strengthen his sense of choice and control.

Revisiting Una (Chapter 4)

Though I put the transcript with Una in Chapter 4 under the section called Keeping the Contract, there are many principles demonstrated in that case that would also be appropriate for the discussion here. Una found herself numb to her grief and other emotions connected to the death of her husband. During her annual months of anniversary reaction, she would feel more anger and depression than grief. The fact that she had never been able to deeply mourn her loss left her feeling burdened by her bereavement ("I'm hoping you can help me take this away"). She vacillated between feeling nothing much of the year and then feeling suffocated by her grief as the anniversary came around. In that session, I could see that her eyes were tense with holding back tears and sadness. For her the key was in finding a rhythm of letting go while still holding on to her good memories and feelings. She identified this herself as the session culminated: "I must learn to take smaller steps."

Epilogue: Life After Trauma

Organizing a trauma memory into an outline (which will be a main topic of the next chapter) basically involves arranging a trauma story as one might to create a book or play. Whether written or acted, many stories include a final chapter or act that looks into the future, often taking place after the actual story has ended. The term for that type of ending is *epilogue*. The application of *epilogues* in trauma treatment provides an additional way in which good memories can be of use in the recovery of traumatized individuals. An epilogue will *not* be appropriate for every trauma history, but it will be helpful to a sufficient number of clients that it is worth considering. In addition, using epilogues has applications in both Phase 1 and Phase 2 trauma treatment. I first introduced this concept in my self-help book, 8 *Keys to Safe Trauma Recovery* (Rothschild, 2010). However, this is the first time I have included a discussion of epilogues in a professional book.

The idea of epilogues gained my interest when I realized that recounts of trauma memories typically end when the incident itself ends. Sometimes that works, but too often it can leave the client in a no-man's land: The trauma ended, now what? From that insight I became interested in the events that *followed* that ending. Of course in some cases, the end of a traumatic incident is just a step in a life filled with ongoing trauma. Under those circumstances, I do not think of the client's trauma story as really having an ending; instead, their traumas just went on and on. In such a circumstance I would *not* recommend introducing the idea of epilogue. However, many clients have trauma stories where the incident or incidents did, truly, end, and life (rather than trauma) went on. In such instances, I prefer to spend time on that more positive outcome, cultivating resources and using the evidence contained in the epilogue to reinforce the fact of their survival.

As a part of Phase 1 trauma treatment, I have often helped a client to process any positive events that followed the traumatic event. Targeting the resources and survival evidence in the epilogue is usually very stabilizing, if sometimes emotional. For example, in helping a middle-aged survivor of a 20-years-past brutal trauma that included a period of captivity, we spent periodic sessions focusing on her subsequent marriage, the birth of her children, the job she then loved. In no way did we forget that the horrible and brutal events of two decades earlier had occurred, but by investing energy in how her life actually turned out, the pain of that part of her past lost some of its sting. By focusing on her epilogue, she became better able to stabilize her dysregulation and stop flashbacks. She implemented reminders of her husband, children, good work, current friends, and so on. In doing so, she became more and more able to access her rainbows to soften the impact of those very dark clouds.

When Phase 2 trauma memory resolution is agreed upon, it is often my preference to begin the processing of the memories with the epilogue instead of the events leading up to the traumatic incident. It seems that once the client's awareness of, and belief in, the fact of her survival and the life-affirming events that followed is strengthened, approaching the horrific memories at the core of the trauma becomes much easier to face. Reinforcing the epilogue before working with the traumatic incident itself provides a continual reminder that the traumatic memories the client is facing did, indeed, have an end. Particularly when good support and contact are a part of the epilogue, memories of exactly that can serve as an anchor to mediate the rising stress associated with processing the incident. With many clients I have had them take breaks from reviewing the horrific memories by remembering the contact and support that followed, moving back and forth between memory of the terror and memory of the later comfort (Levine [2010] would call this *pendulation*) until the memory of the trauma fades in comparison to the memory of the resource: the rainbow outshines the clouds.

CHAPTER SEVEN

Pacing, Portioning, and Organizing

The hurrier I go, the behinder I get.

—Lewis Carroll

In my training programs, during lectures, and via individual professional supervision and consultation, the same kinds of questions keep popping up. Problems therapists run into with their clients during courses of trauma treatment have a lot in common. Typical difficulties involve client dissociation, decompensation, avoidance, resistance, and so on. Generally, therapists want help for the clients to better tolerate the severity of trauma therapy and make it easier for them. However, both therapists and clients are often hampered by a need to rush through the work, get it over with as soon as possible. This can be because of external limits set by clinics, health care agencies, employee assistance, and insurance companies. It can also be due to internal pressures from client, therapist, or both. Over the years, the fixes for these problems—though, of course, with individual variation—fall into a few general categories:

- Greater attention to Phase 1 stabilization and safety
- Reapportioning and reprioritizing steps in the therapy process
- Organizing a trauma memory for easier and more organized Phase 2 work

The first point was addressed at length in the first chapter of this book. The second and third points will be the focus of this chapter.

The Value of Baby Steps and Experimentation

Over the years I have supervised, been consultant, and answered treatment questions for thousands of trauma therapists. I would estimate that about half of the difficulties that I have been presented with involve pacing that is just too speedy or steps that are simply too large for the client to manage. And despite the fact that I definitely believe in my disclaimer as written in the introduction to this book, I am sure of at least one truth, best expressed by Lewis Carroll in *Alice in Wonderland*:

> *The hurrier I go, the behinder I get.*

Though I would say that was true for most things in life, it is particularly apt in helping traumatized individuals to recover. Time and time again I have witnessed therapists and clients trying to push the recovery process and ending up extending it instead, sometimes severely. It is sort of similar to what happens when someone tries to get active too soon after a serious illness or major surgery and ends up with a relapse, increased exhaustion, needing additional treatment as a result, and so on. There are just some processes that cannot be rushed. Trauma healing is one of them.

In general, any time the client is either regressing or at the least not progressing, instead of assuming resistance, it would be a good idea to look at the pacing of the therapy. If, as a supervisee recently complained, the client looks like she "gets it" in the session, but then cannot follow through on the assignment or apply the insight, consider that the step is too big or the process too quick. A good, general rule of thumb is to set the pacing and the steps to a size and tempo that the client can definitely succeed with. Sometimes that might seem frustratingly small or slow, but I can (nearly) guarantee you that smaller, slower steps lead to bigger and quicker results.

Amanda had been involved in a shooting incident at a supermarket. One of the results was that she was no longer able to do the food shopping for her family. She was just too terrified to walk into *any* grocery store. Her first therapist insisted on in vivo *desensitization*, which involves facing a frightening situation head on. The therapist structured Amanda's return to grocery shopping in steps beginning with driving into the parking lot. Even that was too much for Amanda and she fled the therapy in panic. When she came to see me she agreed that being able to food shop was high on her list of goals for the therapy. But it was clear we had to approach it in a more metered manner. After spending adequate time teaching Amanda to calm her frequent episodes of anxiety and panic, she felt ready to tackle the shopping situation. However, our first steps did not involve her going near to the store at all. Step one, the first step that Amanda was confident she could manage successfully, was merely sitting in the chair in my office and *imagining* writing a grocery list. Even that step caused her to pale and raised her pulse (SNS II), but due to our careful attention to stabilization, she was able to calm herself (PNS II). That was the first time she had been able to even think about supermarket shopping without becoming totally, uncontrollably unglued. Even though that was such a tiny step, Amanda felt encouraged and relieved. She reasoned that if she could manage that first step, it would just be a matter of time before she would manage the next and then the next and so on. She repeated that first step many times until imagining writing her shopping list caused only a slight rise in arousal (SNS I). Then she felt ready for the next step.

I have also heard too many therapists assert that their client, in some way, wrecked what had been a "good therapy session." That usually means that the session appeared to be productive, but in the aftermath the client could not contain what was learned or had seemed to be resolved. It could also be that the client had an adverse reaction such as a panic attack or dissociative episode following the session. My response to such complaints is, "It can't have been a good session if the result was not good, no matter how good it *looked* at the time." When a therapy session has a negative impact, that has to mean that something in the session was just too much for the client. It could be the timing, or the pacing was too much, or that the topic or task was just plain premature. Instead of blaming the client, as is all too common, it would be better for both client and therapist for them to look together at what went awry and backtrack to a place or pace that the client can handle.

It is worth remembering that if clients will not or cannot do something, or if they become too distressed in any attempt, it means they are, in some way, not ready for it. I do not believe that *resistance or avoidance* is the result of being obstinate or stubborn. Instead, to me it translates to mean, "I'm not ready," or "I don't have the tools to cope with this." Just as with any other defense, and as discussed in Chapter 5, these are coping mechanisms and have advantages.

Outlining: Easing Transition From Phase 1 to Phase 2

I briefly introduced the procedure of outlining a trauma memory in *The Body Remembers* (Rothschild, 2000) and applied it to a case example in *The Body Remembers CASEBOOK* (Rothschild, 2003). In the intervening years, the technique and the theory base have become much more sophisticated and nuanced. When applied to its fullest potential, outlining has turned out to not only be a terrific way to structure work with trauma memory—making it possible to process an incident in any order so that more manageable parts can be dealt with before the more difficult—but also a marvelous intervention of its own that can ease the transition from the stabilization work of Phase 1 to the provocative and dysregulating work of Phase 2 memory processing. The case below, in transcript and narration, provides a detailed example of the application of this most useful intervention. It is also worth mentioning that outlining can be used no matter which method is employed for processing trauma memories. It is equally advantageous and effective for structuring trauma memory resolution with EMDR, Prolonged Exposure, Somatic Experiencing, and the like.

As discussed in Chapter 1, any time trauma memories are evoked there is risk of destabilization. That is also true for outlining the memory, even though the disruption should be easier to handle as the outlining is done in small, graduated steps. Nonetheless, it is important to note that outlining a traumatic memory can be destabilizing in itself. Therefore the client needs to be stable enough to tolerate and regulate periods of dysregulation. In order to help ensure that the outlining is a good and bearable experience, some kind of safety valve needs to be agreed on (between client and therapist) first. Usually that means a particularly powerful resource, something that would be called an anchor in Somatic Experiencing or a Safe Place in Eye Movement Desensitization and Reprocessing. It is important that the resource that is chosen for this purpose be something *actual* from a client's life: a place she has been, a person he has known, an activity the client has participated in. That is because, as discussed in the previous chapter, the somatic markers associated with this resource need to be strong enough to antidote any distress provoked in the creation of the outline. Moreover, as discussed above, the outline process should proceed in steps that are small enough to be manageable and digestible for the client.

After the anchor or safe place has been chosen, the therapist guides the client, step by step (as demonstrated below) in developing the outline. Of course the therapist should be monitoring the client's autonomic nervous system (ANS) as described in Chapter 2. Any time the client's level of arousal moves him into the orange, SNS II or higher, discussion of the outline must immediately cease via a switch to the anchor or safe place. The process proceeds in this way, one chapter at a time, until the outline is complete. Naming the steps in the outline (book chapters, acts in a play, tracks on a DVD, and so on) out of order is preferable and helps to facilitate the client feeling in control of the process. It is helpful if the therapist writes down each of the chapters in proper order to keep an overview of it. The client may or may not want a written copy (if he does, make sure he writes it himself). The entire process can be done in a single session with some clients, but it is not unusual for it to take two, three, or more sessions to complete. My advice is to let it take the time it takes, making sure the client is managing the process every step of the way, keeping arousal to the blue SNS I or green PNS II as much as possible.

Phase 2 First Steps: Dylan

Dylan is in his mid-20s. He works as a crane operator on construction projects. He was molested multiple times by a member of the clergy between the ages of 8 and 11. This is something that has haunted him in the years since, particularly affecting his self-worth and intimate relationships. Currently he is single and living by himself. He came to therapy wanting to make peace with his past because of a desire to get married and have children and because flashbacks and anxiety attacks related to that trauma were compromising his safety on his job. These symptoms became worse in the year leading up to his self-referral, triggered by increasing numbers of news stories of similar traumas to young boys. He first tried a psychotherapy clinic that specialized in prolonged exposure therapy, but he found that worsened his symptoms. He came to me via referral from a female friend who had had a successful trauma therapy with me. The first few months of his therapy were focused on Phase 1 stabilization. Though not symptom free, he is now able to stop any flashbacks and calm himself when he becomes anxious. His increased stability has helped him to gain confidence in himself and the therapy process. And his job performance has improved and stabilized. We are in agreement that he is ready to move on to Phase 2 to process and resolve this childhood trauma memories.

Outlining, Session 1

Therapist [T]: Hello Dylan. We agreed last week that you are ready to work with the trauma that brought you to therapy. You have become stable enough to manage your symptoms; you are safe; you have strengthened a couple of your friendships; and you are active in your daily life. Those are all good foundations for moving on from Phase 1 stabilization to Phase 2 trauma memory processing and resolution. Is that what you still want to do?

Dylan [D]: You bet!

    T: How are you feeling about it as we begin to talk about it?

    D: Excited and a little nervous. I want to finally put this behind me.

    T: Last week you also chose an anchor to help to antidote the stress of processing the incident. Do you remember what your anchor is?

    D: Of course! It is my best friend's mother and their house when I was in middle school.

    T: How do you feel just mentioning that now?

    D: Calm. A little sad to no longer be in contact with them. That was such an oasis for me at that time.

Choosing something calming to remember or think about is a common trauma therapy intervention for taking a break and calming the nervous system. Similar strategies are used in nearly every trauma method called by a variety of names. Here I will be using Peter Levine's concept of anchor and pendulation to mediate the stress of remembering the past event (Levine, 2010). The sadness associated with Dylan's memory is not necessarily a hindrance to its value as an anchor. I am looking for what calms a client's nervous system. Some level of sadness or grief, particularly when it is bittersweet as in this case, is often very healing, calming, stabilizing, and "gluing." Monitoring of the client's ANS will serve as my gauge for evaluating and modulating the effect of both trauma memory and anchor. From what I can see and hear, Dylan's arousal is in the green PNS II range of calm. So this is a good kind of sadness, and will be useful in helping to mediate or antidote the effects of the traumatic stress elicited by remembering the incidents.

    T: Remind me of your friend's name and what you called his mother.

    D: His name is Sam and I called his mother Mrs. O.

    T: I saw you take a big breath. Did you feel that?

    D: Yes, it's easy to breathe when I think of them.

T: Excellent. Are you ready to go on?

D: Yes, but more nervous. . . .

T: So, before we begin, let me tell you about how we will proceed. I think that might help to put you at ease.

D: Okay.

T: We will not just dive into the memories. First I want to help you organize your memory into an outline. Then we will be able to tackle it one section at a time. That should help to make the processing more digestible and easier to manage. Just a bit at a time rather than all at once.

D: Really? At the other clinic, they told me I had to just remember it all at once if I wanted to resolve it. That scared me so much I left. But now I feel like I could.

T: There are many ways to approach resolving a traumatic memory. My opinion is to make it as easy as possible. Outlining it first has proven to be a good entry for my clients. At any rate, it can't hurt and we can always stop and just dive in if the outlining doesn't suit you. Fair enough?

D: Okay, I'm willing to try it.

Though I don't want Dylan to feel pushed to do the outlining, I am fully convinced it will make processing and resolving his trauma memories much easier for him. Nonetheless, I have given him an out so that he feels he has control over it. I very much doubt he will use the diving-in option.

T: First of all, just to check, do you know what an outline is?

D: Of course, we had to make outlines before we wrote our papers in school.

T: That's a good start. For outlining the memory of your trauma, you can decide if you want to think of it as that kind of school-paper outline, or the chapters in a book's table of contents, an overview of acts in a play, or the list of tracks on a DVD, that kind of thing. What would appeal to you?

D: Well, what happened has always seemed an important story of my life, so how about chapters in a book?

T: Fine with me—that's really up to you.

D: Then I choose chapters in a book.

T: What I will be helping you to do, then, is to decide on a title for the book and then create a table of contents, listing the titles of each chapter. It is important that the titles be brief, only a few words. And that there are not too many chapters. A mistake some people make is to have a lot of chapters, each one really a step in the trauma. When that happens, making the outline is more like reviewing the trauma in detail. In a situation like that, the value of the outlining gets lost. So I am going to help you keep this structured. And one last thing—you don't need to have a title for every chapter right now. Eventually, it's a good idea, but sometimes titles come later. If you know there is a chapter but either don't know the title or don't want to say it yet, we can just put a placeholder for it. Do you have questions?

D: I guess I don't really understand why you want me to make this outline. If you told me, I don't remember.

T: You know what? You are right. I was so busy telling you *how* to do it, I forgot to explain *why* do it. I'm glad you could call me on that!

I am (nearly) always happy when a client can call me on a misstep. Not only do I want to be corrected and avoid a hazard, I also want my client to feel comfortable to do that. I have always seen psychotherapy—and especially trauma therapy—as a partnership of therapist and client. The relationship, as in any course of therapy, is central to a successful outcome. Moreover, since PTSD is much about a person having been and continuing to feel out of control (Rothschild, 2010, pp. 76–77), being open to the client taking the reins where appropriate and safe can be a terrific aid to healing.

T: The outline serves several functions. For one, it organizes and contains the traumatic memory. That helps to reduce the feeling of chaos and being out of control that usually accompanies remembering trauma. And then once the outline is complete, it makes it possible to work with the memory in pieces rather than all at once. All in all, it just helps make resolving trauma memories much easier and more digestible. I've also found it to be a wonderful way to transition from the Phase 1 stabilizing work to the Phase 2 memory resolution work. Have I said too much? Did you follow all that?

D: I think I did. I like the idea of taking it in pieces. I didn't like having to remember it all at once at that clinic. I think I'm ready now.

T: I nearly forgot. . . . As you make this outline, I will also stop you from time to time to remember Sam and Mrs. O. Taking breaks to remember good things will help to ease your nervous system and keep the outlining manageable. So I hope you won't mind when I interrupt you.

D: Like you have done before—interrupt me when I start to get anxious or have a flashback?

T: Exactly.

D: Okay. That always helps.

T: Shall we start?

D: Okay. What do I do first?

T: Since there were multiple incidents of the trauma you will be working with, we need to agree on a single incident at a time to process. You won't be able to work with every occurrence; there were just too many times. Anyway, that isn't necessary. However, you also can't work with all of them at once as that would likely be overwhelming. So you need to pick. It could be the first time, or the last, or the worst one you remember. It could also be a particular time that was typical, if there was such.

This is a common dilemma in helping clients resolve memories of traumas that involve multiple episodes. Incest, sexual abuse, physical abuse, domestic violence, and so on rarely occur only once. So when a client is stable enough to work with his memories, helping to structure the work with outlining, and by also prioritizing which episodes to work with one at a time will help to make the difficult work digestible and easier to integrate. Avoiding overwhelm is a must!

D: In a way, I think many of the times run together. The first and last times stand out more clearly. Which should I choose?

T: Which in your mind and feelings would be *least* challenging?

D: Probably the last time. I was older and bigger and that's when I finally stopped him.

T: That's a terrific idea to start there. Starting at a time when you were able to gather your resources will likely strengthen and reinforce those resources to use in dealing with the earlier incidents. It also can be helpful and healing to begin from the knowledge that this series of abuses did, actually, end. Does that make sense.

D: Yes. I like the idea. I feel nervous but also a little excited to start there.

T: First give your chapter book a title. Remember, just a few words.

D: Uh . . .

T: You don't have to be specific or literal. Just a title that means something to you.

D: Okay. "Him."

T: Now just notice how you feel having titled it.

D: Whew! I'm all sweaty all of a sudden. A little cold.

Cold sweat goes with SNS II, definitely time to hit the brakes.

T: So let that go now and tell me a little about Sam and Mrs. O.

D: Well, Sam was my age and we did lots of things together. I remember we liked to play *Star Wars* in their backyard. Mrs. O was just always really nice to me. She called me her second son.

T: How do you feel remembering that?

D: Better. Warmer. Less sweat. [exhales] I can breathe better.

ANS winding down to blue SNS I, toward green PNS II.

T: I know we just got started, but have you learned anything about this process in these first steps?

D: I'm glad there are steps. Just naming the book title really affected me! I am glad you stopped me to remember my friend. If we'd kept going, I might have had a flashback. Can we really take it *that* slow?

T: Absolutely. I will keep stopping and reminding you of Sam and Mrs. O. But you can also do that yourself, particularly if you feel a break would be good and I haven't noticed yet. We can figure this out together.

D: What if I take too many breaks?

T: I don't think that could happen.

D: You wouldn't worry I was avoiding it?

T: Not at all. I'd be happy you were learning to pace yourself. That will help you outside of here too, in your life. Rarely, an outline gets completed in a single session. More often it takes two or more sessions if it is well paced. So take your time.

In fact, we will end up taking two sessions for this outline.

D: Okay. What now?

T: Are you ready to go on with the outline?

D: Yes.

T: How do you know? What signs are there in your body and your feelings that indicate you are ready?

D: I feel calmer again. And just a little more confident.

Green PNS II, Calm. Good to go on.

T: Excellent. So tell me approximately how many chapters this book has. Usually there are about six to eight, sometimes one or two more or less. Just make a guess now and I will make space for placeholders in my notes. Don't worry if we add or delete one or more later.

I have learned to suggest to clients a limited number of chapters. This helps to create a structure in their minds for keeping the outlining succinct. What I want to avoid is an outline that is really more of a line-by-line detailed narrative of the traumatic incident, such as: (1) The doorbell rang; (2) I answered it; (3) he pushed on the door; (4) I tried to close it; and so on. What is preferable is for the outline to be just that, an outline. That means each point, chapter, or act should be a main idea, not a detail.

D: Probably six or seven.

T: Then I will write the numbers 1 through 7 in my notebook. I'll make sure to leave room in case you find you want to insert another in somewhere. And don't worry about naming all of them today. As we proceed through this, you may find it easier or harder to come up with or say a chapter title. It is absolutely fine to skip one or more. If you do that, I'll make sure there is a placeholder. By the way, I usually write an outline in my notes and keep it from session to session. You are welcome to use the paper and clipboard beside you on the table to write it also. That is completely up to you. Some clients like to have a copy; some prefer I keep it for them. And, again, you don't have to decide that now; that option is open on an ongoing basis.

D: Thanks, for now I'm happy for you to keep track of it.

T: How are you feeling right now as we are proceeding?

D: I feel okay. This seems manageable, if a little slow.

PNS I, calm. Good to go on.

T: You are right, I prefer to do this slowly.

D: It's sort of strange as I felt so pushed at the other clinic. But I feel like I can keep up with you better.

T: Glad to hear that. Are you ready to name a chapter title?

D: Yes.

T: Which one do you want to name first? It is probably a good idea to name one that is less hard and save the most difficult for later.

D: Really? Not get the worst over with?

T: Not in my experience, though others might disagree. And that will apply as we work with the outline also. Working with the less tough bits first should help you to get used to working with the memories and gain ability and confidence. If we pace it well, by the time you get to the worst parts, they will be much easier to deal with than you feel they would be right now.

D: Okay. I'll try it your way. It makes sense to me.

T: So which chapter first?

D: The last one: "Slamming the Door."

T: What happens when you name that?

D: Relieved. I like that we are getting started. And I like the finality of that chapter title.

T: How is that in your body?

D: I feel like I can breathe. And, funny, I feel sort of strong in my arms.

T: Nice.

PNS I, calm. Good to go on. Here's a good example of the payoff of comprehensive Phase 1 work so that the client is stable before diving into trauma memory, and also of the value of structuring the entry into the Phase 2 work. Whereas Dylan was nervous to proceed to processing his trauma, he is now feeling calm, relieved, and strong. That doesn't mean that he won't hit some thorny areas and feelings. But it is a good start that lays a secure foundation for the difficult work ahead. He goes into it much better equipped to traverse that tough territory.

T: Are you ready then to name another chapter title?

D: Yes, I think so. . . . The first chapter would be: "The Choir."

T: What's happening after you name that chapter?

D: My stomach is tight. I'm remembering how it felt to go to choir. . . . My parents made me continue. . . .

SNS II, edging toward flight/fight. Increased stomach tension. I can see he's holding his breath. Good time for brakes.

T: I'm going to stop you there. We are not yet processing your memory, just naming the chapters. So I am stopping you from going further into it. Just naming it, for right now, is provocative enough.

D: [exhales]

T: I see you exhaling. What's going on?

D: I'm sort of relieved that you stopped me. I started to feel like the memory was taking over.

T: And now?

D: I can breathe a little better.

SNS I, safely back to active/alert. Good to go on. It is critically important to maintain the contract that we are outlining and not processing. If I don't hold that boundary, the containment and resource gathering benefits of outlining will be lost and flashback or overwhelm (as was beginning to happen here) could result. We will get to the processing, but in a structured manner and after Dylan has finished the outline.

T: Good. Let's switch here and take a break to remember your friend and his mother.

D: Yes, I want to go back there now.

T: Oops, wait a minute. We have to be clear and honest here. You cannot "go back" there—either to your friend and his mother or to the incident we are outlining. It is important to be just as clear and firm when remembering good incidents as with bad ones. What you are able to do is to *remember* them. Neither the good memories nor the bad ones can be "revisited" or "relived," only remembered.

D: But it is nice to *feel like* I am there.

T: I get that, but it could be dangerous to think of it that way. If you believe you can be back in that house with your friend, how will you distinguish that you can*not* be back in the room with the minister?

D: Oh! I see your point. If I believe I can be back in the one, it would confuse me about the other. Okay, I'll try it your way. . . . I want to *remember* being with Sam and Mrs. O.

This is another critical point. It is vitally important to distinguish that processing a trauma memory or even having a flashback is a phenomenon of memory, not time travel. It is very common for both clients and their therapists to talk about "reliving," "revisiting," "being back there," or "going back there." That kind of language will make it much more difficult for the client to recognize that the trauma is over exactly because it is now, not then.

T: What about them would you like to remember right now?

D: I'm remembering when Sam got a retriever puppy for his 10th birthday. He was so excited. I was too, but also a little envious. Sam said that he'd share the dog with me and wanted me to help him name it. That was so cool. I felt like we were brothers.

T: How are you feeling right now?

D: Much more calm. The tension in my stomach is gone.

PNS I, calm. Good to go on.

T: Are you ready to name another chapter?

D: Yes, I think so. Chapter 2 is "After the Service."

T: And how are you feeling?

D: Okay . . . but I know what's coming next. I want to name the next chapter now.

T: Okay.

D: "Over My Shoulder."

T: And how is that?

D: I feel a little shaky. It is hard not to go further in my memory, but I am trying to stop it like you told me to.

SNS I, active/alert. He has some distress, but is able to act in his own interest. Good to go on.

T: That's terrific for you to practice stopping yourself. That will help you now, and later too. Can you tell me more about Sam and the puppy?

D: Sure. I'd never had a puppy myself, so it was really fun. He was so cute, so curious. And he loved to lick our faces. We'd run with him and teach him tricks. All that boy and dog stuff. It was a really good time. When I spent the night, the puppy (and later when he was grown) would alternate between sleeping with Sam and with me. It really did seem that he knew Sam shared him with me [smiling].

T: You have a big smile on your face.

D: It's a very happy memory!

T: Are you beginning to see how the good memory you chose anti-dotes the traumatic memory?

D: It really is amazing. I didn't know I could so easily counteract those upsetting feelings. And I really like remembering them all. Makes me want to get on Facebook and see if I can find Sam.

T: Why not?

D: That wouldn't hurt the work I'm doing?

T: I wouldn't think so. . . . I've had clients do that before with car-ing people they remembered in therapy. Sometimes they can't find someone. But when they do it is usually a happy reunion—whether or not they end up spending in-person time together.

D: Then I might try it.

I will admit that I am curious if Sam or his mother knew about the incidents that Dylan is now working with. But in the same way they advise lawyers: Don't ask a question you don't know the answer to. For one, asking now would betray the outlining contract by going into details. And since I don't know if they knew, I also don't know what effect that knowledge would have on Dylan, for better or worse. Therefore, I will need to contain my curiosity, at least for now, maybe for the rest of Dylan's therapy. Perhaps at some point he will volunteer that information. Until then, I can't ask that question unless I am fairly certain it would be helpful to him.

T: It's getting toward time to end this session. Is this an okay stopping point for you?

D: Yes, it's okay.

T: What will you take with you today, what you've gained or learned from this session?

D: I feel better than I thought I would. I guess it is a good thing to make the outline and do it this slowly, even if I just want to get it over with. I guess I'd rather feel good at the end of a slower session than bad at the end of a quicker-paced one.

Nearly always I will ask such a question at the end of a session. This is part of Phase 3, integration: what is the take-home from therapy, the bridge between the session and the client's daily life.

At the second outlining session, Dylan finished the outline using the same procedure as described above. In my notes I have written:

Anchor: Sam & Mrs. O.
Title: Him
1) The choir
2) After the service
3) Over my shoulder
4) Threat
5) Crying
6) No more

7) Slamming the door

The epilogue: Moving on

It is my bent to keep the outline in my notes unless and until the client wants a copy. In that event, I ask the client to write it down himself rather than handing him the list. There is no real theoretical reason for this. It has just never felt comfortable for me to write it for the client. Some clients eventually want their outline to take home; some never do and are happy for me to "hold it" for them.

Once the outline is completed, working with it one chapter at a time can proceed with whichever processing method is chosen by therapist and client. Not only is it not necessary to work with the chapters in order, it is actually often preferable to work with them *out of order*. And, though it does not always happen, I have found that beginning with the epilogue, if there is one, or with the last chapter, whichever best confirms that the trauma—whatever it was—actually did end, to be very advantageous. Do not be surprised if once that final chapter is processed, the traumatic stress bound in the rest of the trauma memory falls away and does not need processing. I have seen this happen repeatedly (though not always) with my own clients and clients of my supervisees and students. It is wonderful to share the excitement and relief of clients when they realize that the events they have feared and suffered with for so long have lost their sting and no longer have power over them.

CHAPTER EIGHT

Adapting Mindfulness, MBSR, and Yoga for Those With PTSD

Mindfulness is simply being aware of what is happening right now without wishing it were different; enjoying the pleasant without holding on when it changes (which it will); being with the unpleasant without fearing it will always be this way (which it won't).

—James Baraz and Michele Lilyana (2016)

The term *mindfulness* is most commonly associated with disciplines of meditation. It usually refers to the practice of purposefully paying attention to, for instance, the sensation of breathing, the feel and taste of a bite of food, or the sound of an internally repeated mantra. Integral to mindfulness is that the attention must be held on something that is occurring in the present moment, *not* thoughts or images of the past or future. In addition, one must hold attention *without* judgment of any feelings or thoughts that arise, and with compassion for, among other things, just how difficult it is to keep your focus in one place. The core mechanism of mindfulness involves attention to a target of awareness, traditionally following the breath in and out. The idea is to notice when your mind wanders to thoughts, feelings, or body sensations and to keep bringing your awareness back to the mindful target. In this way, your mind becomes trained to access and maintain focus in *the present moment,* accepting what is. This simple procedure is thousands of years old and is practiced in all corners of the world by people of all races and beliefs (religious and not). As such, mindfulness is the foundation of meditation practices of all sorts. At this writing, hard research on mindfulness and PTSD is limited. There is nothing available that points to definitive conclusions. Therefore, we must rely heavily on common sense, compassion, anecdotal experiences, observations, and—most importantly—feedback from each and every student and client. However, truth be told, that is what I would advocate even if there were thousands of studies available. Ask your clients what helps and what hurts; supporting them to know themselves is a core benefit of mindfulness.

The increasing popularity of mindfulness and mindfulness practices such as yoga and meditation have facilitated its infiltration into all corners of the helping professions including psychotherapy and trauma treatment. While most would agree that all of these disciplines are useful for traumatized individuals, many have noticed that there can be significant limitations for that population. It is my hope that inclusion of this chapter will alert trauma therapists and mindfulness teachers alike to the inherent difficulties experienced by those who suffer from dysregulated nervous systems. Mindfulness has great potential for antidoting the effects of PTSD. Moreover, it is necessary for safe Phase 2 work, enabling the client to maintain a mindful dual awareness of then and now such that she is able to remember trauma while secure in the knowledge she is in the therapy room with her therapist. I will be suggesting and demonstrating simple fixes and adjustments that temper the difficulties and make mindful practices available and successful for individuals suffering from trauma and PTSD.

The first applications of mindfulness in the psychotherapy field appeared in *Gestalt therapy*, the method developed and popularized by Fritz Perls (1942). That may come as a surprise to many because Gestalt is most known for the *empty chair technique* as created by Perls (1968). Actually, however, the core of Gestalt therapy involves keeping one's awareness in the present by observing what is going on in mind, body, and emotions. Noticing how those change from moment to moment, forming the foundation of this method of personal growth. The Gestalt exercise "Now I am aware" will be familiar to both practitioners of Gestalt and practitioners of mindfulness. Jon Kabat-Zinn (1990) brought mindfulness into the medical world with his book *Full Catastrophe Living*, in which he advocated for the use of mindfulness to enhance coping with stress and catastrophic illness. And then in 1993, Marsha Linehan introduced mindfulness into the mainstream of psychotherapy via her work with and writing on the treatment of borderline personality disorder. Since the early 1990s, the popularity of mindfulness in the treatment of all sorts of psychological conditions has become widespread.

Applying the use of mindfulness to the treatment of post-traumatic stress disorder (PTSD) should be a no-brainer. The present-moment focus of mindfulness is an obvious natural antidote for PTSD, a condition where the mind and body of the trauma survivor are continually wrenched into memories of a terrifying past (i.e., a flashback), which is the core symptom of PTSD. Since mindfulness pulls the attention away from the past and into the here and now, one would think that the two would be a match made in heaven. And it is true that applications of mindfulness practice are spreading across the trauma treatment landscape in the hope of helping those with PTSD. However, unfortunately and a little surprisingly, mindfulness is not always helpful to those with PTSD and may even cause further dysregulation. Teachers of meditation, yoga, Mindfulness-Based Stress Reduction (MBSR), chi gong, tai chi, and other mindfulness-based practices recognize that a significant portion of students who endure PTSD (and also a good many suffering from anxiety and panic) do not always do so well with a mindful focus—at least as traditionally taught in those programs. Nonetheless, *all* of these practices hold plenty of promise for trauma survivors and others with anxiety-based disorders. Modified by adjustments such as varying sensory focus, metering exposure, and helping individuals to tailor any mindfulness-based program to their specific needs, mindfulness can and does fulfill its promise of greater calm and peace of mind, also for people with these challenges. You might be asking: What kinds of risks could something as benign as mindfulness pose? It has been noted that mindfulness practices such as meditation and yoga can trigger dissociation, anxiety, even panic in some participants (Rankin, 1978; Garden, 2007; Booth, 2014; Wylie, 2015). The discussion below will illustrate how some of these risks can come about and also make suggestions for easy, adaptable fixes.

Experiencing Mindfulness-Based Stress Reduction (MBSR)

Some years ago, during a particularly stressful time in my life, I signed on for a local MBSR class. My intention in attending was purely personal. However, it was somewhat impossible to leave my professional self completely at home. So I negotiated with myself to allow professional observation at the same time as I participated fully as a student.

My personal background includes periodic bouts of PTSD, and I have shared bits of my experiences previously (Rothschild, 2010). In general, a majority of trauma professionals come to this field because of their own trauma history or that of friends or family members. For the most part, we are a field of wounded healers. As one myself, I hoped MBSR would contribute to my own stabilization, stress management, and trauma healing. And to a large extent, that was the case. I would recommend MBSR, with provisions to be discussed below, to just about anyone who wanted to use mindfulness to mediate their stress. However, I found that the program could particularly be enhanced by a few specific and targeted adjustments for people with PTSD as well as anxiety and panic disorders. Once my 8 weeks were completed, I approached the teacher, Dr. Christiane Wolf, and asked if she would be interested in meeting and discussing my observations. She enthusiastically agreed, and that was the beginning of a friendship and professional collaboration that continues today. That initial meeting led to my taking the MBSR course for a second time, specifically as a participant-observer to identify how the structure and practice could be strengthened for those with dysregulated nervous systems. Wolf was very open to my observations and feedback from my professional and personal viewpoints as someone who both wrestled with PTSD herself and also helped others so challenged. Wolf had already noticed that certain students struggled with the MBSR program, becoming anxious, falling asleep, dissociating, and so on in reaction to some of the tasks. And she knew that there was a percentage of her students who dropped out before completing the course. She wanted to be able to better help students in those categories. Eventually our meetings led to the development and implementation of a pilot MBSR group specifically tailored to considerations of PTSD, anxiety, and panic (to be discussed below).

The MBSR structure as developed by Jon Kabat-Zinn (1990) consists of eight weekly 2-hour classes. The core of the course is the instruction and practice of meditation, yoga, and a technique called *body scan*. Students make a commitment and are expected to practice these skills on a daily basis throughout the course. Each week there are also lectures on varying mindfulness-based techniques for stress management.

Kabat-Zinn placed the body scan at the beginning of the course to teach the foundations of developing a mindfulness practice. It consists of focused awareness to track body sensations in a structured procedure from top to bottom or bottom to top. Body scan is also a main feature of other meditation disciplines. The common position for the scan is lying down, sometimes with legs and feet supported on a chair, and the process typically takes from 30 to 45 minutes.

I found some difficulty with the structure of the body scan, both personally and professionally, in three areas: the forced nature of it, the length of the scans, and the body position. When Wolf introduced the body scan in the first class, she said of the daily practice, "You don't have to like it, you just have to do it." As previously discussed, PTSD has a lot to do with feelings of loss of control. Being required to practice *any* method with no room for alteration or protest went against the grain of my personal preference, my professional knowledge, and my common sense. In later discussions with Wolf, I understood that she (and Kabat-Zinn) believed that requiring the practice would eventually make it friendly and accessible. I thought the opposite. Moreover, people who suffer with PTSD, anxiety, and panic often have very unpleasant body sensations that they contend with on a daily basis. Being forced to hang out with them in a structured manner for 30 to 45 minutes daily can prove intolerable. In addition, such concentrated body attention carries the risk of triggering a trauma flashback. In fact, Kabat-Zinn (1990, pp. 79–80) discusses a dramatic example of just that. Last, I find my mind much more prone to wander when lying down. And I observed many of the class students falling asleep during the lengthy body scans. Wolf was very open to my feedback and we wondered if it was possible to offer flexible options for body scan pacing (briefer doses) and positioning (sitting on the floor or in a chair, or standing), and, if so, what effect that might have for better or worse.

My concern about positioning and timing also extended to meditation practice. Much of it was done sitting on the floor with legs crossed. That position is no longer possible for my aging and arthritic knees, so I sat in a chair—the only one in the class to do so. But that made me wonder what effect it might have for people to be able to choose their own position for meditation. In addition, meditation segments were usually 30 minutes long. Some in the group reported spacing out or dissociating. And many were frustrated that they could not keep a mindful focus for such a long period of time. This led to further discussion with Wolf concerning more position options and shorter meditation segments, at least at the start, and particularly with those who suffered from PTSD, anxiety, and panic.

Not every body is suited to any one form of exercise or movement. Mine has never been suited to yoga. I have several hypermobile joints, endure knee and shoulder arthritis, and, as I get older, joint stiffness increases. Some yoga postures are just plain out of my reach, and others are torturous because of the time required to hold them. Just not my cup of tea, as they say. However, I know it is wonderful for a lot of people. I have friends, colleagues, students, clients, old and young, who swear by it. I am envious; I wish I could too. That being the case, during the yoga sessions I felt a bit of an outsider. At least at that time, the MBSR program and culture did not have much room for individual variation, so during those sections I was on my own. That was manageable. However, I do have a more general concern about yoga with regard to students with PTSD, anxiety, and panic. As will be discussed in the next section, there are a portion of people with these conditions who do not do well emotionally with the stretching aspect of yoga. For some of these people, yoga stretching risks ungluing them emotionally (Rothschild, 2003).

The final matter that gave me pause—and will be discussed at length below—involves the traditional mindfulness and meditation focus of paying attention to one's breathing. Probably the most common meditation instruction is, "Follow your breath. Notice when you breathe in. Notice when you breathe out." Respiration as a point of focus is fine for me. However, I know that feeling breathing and heart rate can be provoking for some with PTSD. That is because during traumatic experiences respiration and pulse can become very rapid in order to send large amounts of oxygen into the muscles to facilitate flight or fight. So paying attention to breathing and heart rate is often triggering. I questioned, what could be done about that?

I discovered that I am not alone in my concerns. In addition to the articles cited above, online meditation program reviews as well as a good many blogger entries confirm that many have had adverse reactions to meditation or yoga. Another of my colleagues, David Treleaven, became so concerned he investigated such problems for his PhD dissertation and is publishing a book on the topic (in press).

Preventing Potential Aversive Effects of Mindfulness Practices

Valuable as they are, as discussed above, mindfulness-based programs such as MBSR, meditation, and yoga can precipitate undesirable reactions in many of those with PTSD. The good news is that these adverse effects can, for the most part, be prevented with fairly simple adjustments. The areas of highest risk involve:

- Rigidity of program structure or task instructions
- The traditional inward focus of mindfulness targets
- The length of mindfulness sessions and practice
- Postural positions normally assumed during mindfulness, meditation, and yoga practice

- The possibility of relaxation-induced anxiety for some students who have PTSD, or anxiety and panic disorders

Easy fixes for each of these will be discussed below.

Increasing Individual Control and Mastery

Every individual is the best expert on himself and each has the capacity to know what is best at any moment in time. However, sometimes one might not be able to or know how to access this critical information. Mindfulness is actually a terrific tool for helping someone to zero in on what he already knows.

A rather handy tool toward this end is the *mindful gauge* (Rothschild, 2010) that can be used purposefully to recognize what is and is not helpful or desirable in all sorts of circumstances. You may already be very aware of your own mindful gauges—the internal signals you use to make decisions. For instance: How do you know what you want to order from a dinner menu? Is it a thought ("I should have more vegetables today"), a sensation (increased hunger), a behavior (mouth watering as you eye a particular item), or an emotion (I feel happy seeing that apple pie)? Paying attention may help you to identify one or more mindful gauges that might be useful in other situations as well.

A mindful gauge can be, as above, a thought, sensation, a behavior, an emotion, or even an image—identification of these five specific elements inspired by Levine's SIBAM model (Levine, 2010; Rothschild, 2000, 2003). For example, a client of mine had a visual image as her mindful gauge. She would see a rabbit in her mind's eye. The rabbit's demeanor would change depending on what was being decided, looking happy when it seemed a good way to go and sad or scared when it did not (Rothschild, 2010). Any one or a combination of these elements (thought, sensation, behavior, emotion, or image) can be used to help a client tune into her own mindful gauge, though, for some, it may take practice to develop a gauge as a reliable resource.

Another aspect of control and mastery when practicing mindfulness and meditation concerns the eyes. Traditionally, unless engaging in a walking meditation, mindful procedures are usually practiced with eyes closed. Of course closing the eyes while meditating can be helpful to many as that would shut out possibly distracting visual stimuli. However, for someone with PTSD, closing the eyes, especially if required, may increase feelings of not being safe, even fear of imminent danger. Allowing the option of keeping eyes open can make a huge difference in this regard. Just the fact of being able to *choose* can be empowering for a trauma survivor. In addition, if fear for safety is an issue, keeping eyes open will make possible moment-to-moment reassurance that (when it is actually the case) the situation is safe. Moreover, there is no reason that having the eyes open need detract from the benefits of mindfulness and meditation. On the contrary, practicing with open eyes provides an opportunity to train the mind to maintain the targeted focus in spite of possible visual distractions.

Bringing Balance to the Sensory Nervous System

As discussed in Chapter 3, there are two categories of senses corresponding to the two branches of the sensory nervous system. One, the *exteroceptors*, is associated with "the five senses," the sensations we tend to be most familiar with: sight, hearing, taste, touch, and smell. The other, the *interoceptors*, includes less recognized sensations including the vestibular sense (balance) and proprioception (internal body sensations and the ability to locate your body in space). Following the breath, which is a common mindfulness focus, relies on awareness of interoceptors—feeling the breathing from the inside.

Remember, those with PTSD (as well as anxiety and panic) may be fairly used to being overwhelmed by interoceptive sensations. Moreover, increases in respiration and heart rate, as well as dizziness (all interoceptive) are often triggers to PTSD flashbacks because these same sensations are often experienced during, or in the wake of, a traumatic incident. All told, focusing on interoceptors for mindfulness practice can be quite uncomfortable, even provoking, for many a trauma survivor.

Changing the mindful target from interoceptor to exteroceptor, or alternating between the two, can make a huge difference for someone with PTSD. The focus can stay on the breath (when that is tradition or requirement) but instead of feeling it from the inside out, one could try listening to the sound of it or watching the chest go up and down. Alternatively, one could use the exteroceptive visual sense to find something to look at in the current environment, or the auditory sense to locate a sound to attend to, and so on. Another possibility is to practice shifting between an interoceptive sense and an exteroceptive sense: *I feel my breath; I see the poster on the wall; my heart beats faster; I hear the truck outside*; and so on.

Portions, Pacing, and Positions

Traditionally, meditation is practiced in segments of 30 minutes or more at a time. MBSR usually involves 30–45-minute body scans, in addition to sitting and walking meditations. For many with PTSD, these lengths of time are just too long. Allowing individuals to move in and out of meditations and other mindful exercises at *their own pace* can make practice sessions much more accessible to many. An important rule of thumb is to help someone to achieve what they *can*, not push them into ranges where they cannot; *build on success*. Mini-meditations and abbreviated body scans, say for 5 minutes or less at a time, will help the client with PTSD to feel success rather than failure and allow her to *gradually* acclimate to longer periods of time. Toward this end, Christiane Wolf has made abbreviated meditations and scans as well as exteroceptive-focused meditations available on her website (http://www.christianewolf.com/guided-audio-meditations/).

Another important area to consider is which posture or position to assume during mindful practices. It is usual to meditate sitting cross-legged on the floor and to do a body scan lying down. However, either of these positions will not be optimal for everyone. Lying down, in particular, can increase anxiety or dissociation in many with PTSD. There are so many other options; it is easy to help someone find his own best position for mindful practice. In fact, a mindful focus and use of the mindful gauge will identify what is best for an individual at a particular point in time. Have your client choose a position to start with and then, using mindful awareness, evaluate whether that position increases or decreases the ability to stay present, calm, feeling solid or whole, and so on. When a position aids those states, that would indicate a good choice. But if, instead, the client feels spacey, anxious, or diffuse, that position would best be avoided—at least at that moment. Monitoring those same indications during a meditation practice could also serve as a guide to when it is time to take a break or shift position.

Relaxation, Yoga, and PTSD

There can be an additional complication when a mindfulness practice facilitates relaxation. Mindfulness, meditation, and yoga can all increase relaxation in mind and body—and many engage in those practices for just that reason, to be able to relax. Yoga, in addition, involves periods of muscle stretching that further enhance relaxation. However, for individuals with PTSD as well as those plagued by anxiety and panic, these same practices can actually increase distress rather than alleviate it. How could relaxation, something usually sought after, regarded as pleasant, and associated with calmness, be a problem?

About 4% of the general population have been reported to become more anxious when engaging in relaxation training, progressive relaxation, and yoga (Lehrer & Woolfolk, 1993). The phenomenon is called *relaxation-induced anxiety* (Heide & Borkovec, 1983; Mental Health Daily, 2015). There are no specifics available as to who this 4% comprises, but experience points to people with PTSD as well as anxiety and panic disorders as being the most likely candidates. No one really knows why this phenomenon occurs, but it is probably safe to speculate that, for some people, looser muscles feel less secure and less emotionally contained than firmer muscles. The result is that for many with these conditions, aiming for states of *calm* (as identified in the autonomic nervous system) will be more beneficial than striving for *relaxation* (a function of the somatic nervous system). Even though it seems counterintuitive, for many in these circumstances, maintaining, and even increasing, muscle tone enhances calm (Rothschild, 2000).

Many (maybe even most) people with PTSD will probably benefit from yoga; however, avoiding the postures that emphasize stretching muscles and keeping to the poses and procedures that increase muscle strength and balance will probably have the higher chance of success with this population.

In *The Body Remembers CASEBOOK* (Rothschild, 2003, pp. 212–217), I wrote at length about my client Thomas and how we adapted the yoga he was doing to a more optimal program for him. Though he had an extensive trauma background, he first contacted me for help when his symptoms of emotional instability became more acute. Concurrently he had also developed problems with his joints. In taking a careful history which included his current life situation and activities, I discovered that he had begun practicing yoga shortly before the onset of those symptoms that motivated him to contact me. The timing of symptom onset was suspicious. As Thomas realized the direction of my thoughts, he became very upset. He loved his yoga practice and was afraid I was going to tell him to stop doing it. If I did, he threatened, he would not come back to therapy with me. First I reassured him that forbidding yoga was not at all on my agenda even though I did see a connection. Once he calmed down and could listen, I told him that I agreed that the yoga was good for him, for the most part, but that there might be one or more postures or procedures that might need adjustment. I asked if he would be interested in tailoring his yoga program to maximize the benefits and minimize the negative impact. Yes, of that he was sure. So we spent subsequent sessions working with mindful awareness (body and emotions) as he showed me the various poses they assumed in his classes. One by one we investigated the effect a pose had on him emotionally and on his joints. Eventually we found that there were three positions that he had to strike from his program, but the rest were mostly fine. His yoga teacher was enthusiastic to help him to make minor adjustments to a few of the remaining poses to maximize emotional and joint stability. These same principles of applying mindful awareness to a practice of yoga, meditation, martial arts—exercise of any sort—can be implemented to maximize the benefits and reduce adverse effects.

Exteroceptive Mindfulness Reduces Dissociation: Faith

Following Faith's survival of an apartment house fire in which one of her neighbors died, she found it difficult to concentrate at work. Her thoughts were constantly pulled into the memories of that horrible night, and ruminations of what she could have done differently. Intellectually she knew that she had done all that was possible and that the neighbor's own cigarette had been the culprit. Nonetheless, 6 months later she was still plagued by flashbacks and obsessive thoughts. We were agreed that taking control of these symptoms was integral to the Phase 1 goal of stabilization. What she most wanted was to be free of the flashbacks and the torturous ruminations. Prior to the fire she had been enthusiastic about and engaged in meditation practice; however, now, when she tried to meditate in the ways she had done previously, she could not maintain her focus. She was frustrated and concerned to lose what had been such a useful resource for her. If I could help her to reclaim her ability to meditate, she pleaded, and get back control of her mind, she would be most grateful.

The traditional inward focus of mindfulness no longer worked for Faith. Focusing on her breath made it too easy for her mind to wander to the memory of smoke and the tragedy it signified. That led me to wonder if she had lost the facility for meditation altogether or if it was the focus, the target, that was at issue. This was simple enough to test. I briefly taught her about the difference between exteroceptors and interoceptors. She caught on easily. In the session we tried a few mini-meditations, a few minutes each, testing out a variety of exteroceptive targets: a picture on my wall, the sound of the traffic outside the window, her sense of touch as she rubbed her hands on her denims.

Faith was surprised and encouraged to find that she could maintain focus on an exteroceptive sense for the short durations we tested. She wanted to go further with this and we agreed she would make experiments in the intervening week, trying out different exteroceptive targets and a variety of longer and shorter time structures. She came back the next week much calmer. She had been able to have significant periods free of flashback and troubled thoughts as she gradually increased her exteroceptive meditation time. In addition, she found (what she thought was) a surprising and clever exteroceptive target: the smell of peppermint. She wanted to find something she could sniff when she was reminded of the smoke from the fire. The next time she was triggered, she happened to have a roll of mints in her purse. In desperation, she pulled them out and took a good whiff. She steadied nearly instantly as that aroma quickly drew her attention into the present moment and away from the memory of the fire's smoke. After that she often used a pack of mints as her mindful meditation target. None of this was a cure for her PTSD in itself, but gaining back the resource of mindfulness, and increasing her control over meditation practice and her symptoms, greatly facilitated her stabilization and improved her daily life. That paved the way for our further work together.

Pilot Group: MBSR Tailored for PTSD

Taking all of the issues discussed above into consideration, in 2013 Dr. Christiane Wolf and I teamed up to develop a pilot MBSR program specifically aimed at the special needs of individuals with PTSD. It was a small self-funded group, but gave us the chance to test some of our hypotheses about what might help make mindfulness more accessible for those with PTSD. For the most part, our hunches were accurate for this group. Reducing the durations of meditations and body scans made both procedures much more comfortable and successful for the participants. In addition, giving them the option of an exteroceptor-based target greatly increased their ability to stay mindfully focused. The one surprising result was that most of them found the mindful gauge to be the most valuable tool they acquired during the program. When time and funding allow, we definitely hope to further develop, monitor, and write about PTSD-tailored MBSR programs.

Mindful Self-Care for the Professional

It is worth noting (if briefly) that mindfulness can be an important adjunct to self-care for trauma therapists and helping professionals. Actually, it may be their first and best line of defense. There is a small, but growing body of data that indicates that trauma professionals who practice mindfulness during therapy sessions have lowered rates of vicarious trauma, compassion fatigue, and burnout (Harrison, 2007; Thompson, Amatea, & Thompson, 2014). This does not mean that one needs to constantly be mindful when working with clients (though that is not a bad idea). All it seems to require is periodically checking in with oneself. When you ask your client about the temperature of her hands, check yours too. When you notice your client's breathing, pay attention to yours. And so on. Also, monitoring your own ANS arousal, per the color table accompanying and discussed in chapter 2, will also be a great help in limiting your own adverse risks. Just make sure to put on the brakes when *your* arousal is getting too high and threatening your ability to think clearly.

Here are a couple of tasks you can try. If you find them useful, practice will ensure they are available to you whenever you need them.

1. When you are with your client, check in with yourself at regular intervals. You might set a soft alarm on your phone or invest in a meditation type of alarm clock (they chime at programmed intervals). Do not worry about this disrupting your clients, as it is just as good for them to also check in with themselves at regular intervals.
2. When you are with your client, periodically notice if you can keep mindful awareness of yourself and your client *at the same time.* Usually therapists are more aware of their clients than of themselves. Nevertheless, with practice, you can learn to tune in to both, either simultaneously or sequentially.

These are both exercises I offer in self-care trainings to good result. If you would rather gain facility with these before trying when you are with your clients, arrange to practice with one or more colleagues.

Empathy Dial

Empathy is definitely a good resource to have as a psychotherapist. However, as with anything else, it can be too much of a good thing. As I discussed at length in *Help for the Helper* (Rothschild, 2006), empathy has a double edge. It helps you to resonate and relate to your clients, but it is also the mechanism that puts you at risk for compassion fatigue and vicarious traumatization. That does not mean that you need to stop being empathetic in order to protect yourself. There are degrees of empathy, and you can learn to adjust your level of empathy just as you can adjust your levels of arousal. Think of your empathy as having a control dial like the volume dial on an old-fashioned stereo, radio, or television. You may need to imagine an older version as many modern ones do not have dials anymore. They used to look something like this:

Most of you will *not* need instruction in how to turn your empathy dial up. Helping professionals of all types, including psychotherapists, are usually very strong on empathy, often too strong. That is why, I believe, we are at such high risk for compassion fatigue and vicarious traumatization. However, learning strategies and tricks to monitor and adjust your empathy dial can be very handy. Then, at the least, you will have a choice from situation to situation, of whether it is most advantageous—and the best care for yourself—to turn your dial up or down. Turning it up means you resonate more strongly emotionally, somatically, and intuitively with your client; turning it down will give you increased professional objectivity and clearer thinking. Mindfulness will be your best tool to evaluate the degree of your empathy at any point in time, and whether turning it up or down would be most beneficial. Then mindfulness will help you to know when adjustments are warranted or advantageous.

The most straightforward mechanism for turning down your empathy dial is simply to feel the support and seat of your chair, or, if you are sitting forward (as many do with clients), to lean back so that you are touching the back of your chair and can feel the back and seat. Giving yourself the directive "sit back" from time to time will help you with this. Pay attention mindfully to notice if sitting back gives you more "breathing space" and room to think. Also pay mindful attention to your client and see if sitting back has a desirable or adverse effect. Usually you will find the client also gets more breathing space when you turn down your empathy dial in this way.

Other helpful mechanisms include paying attention to your own facial expression, respiration rhythm, and your body posture to monitor that you are not mirroring the same in your client. Facial, respiratory, and postural mirroring are very quick to drive the empathy dial way up (Rothschild, 2006). That can be useful in short spurts, but is not recommended for long periods. In general, mindfulness will help you to monitor your empathy dial, enabling you to reduce the risk of negative effects from your work.

Trauma Therapist Beware

Avoiding Common Hazards

Everybody makes mistakes. Me too! Too little sleep, not feeling well, a conflict with a friend or partner, too much to do in too little time, internal pressures such as one's own trauma issues, worries such as financial difficulties or a child's problem at school all can preoccupy and impact a therapist's attention, clear thinking, and patience. And while no one wants their own stresses to impact their clients, it happens. There are additional errors made from misunderstanding, or too little, or incomplete information. And even more as the result of sticking with something you believe to be true that turns out not to be so—at least for that client at that moment. It also helps to keep in mind that as knowledge evolves, what once was standard procedure may now be seen as a mistake and vice versa. Many of these situations that produce clinical errors are unavoidable, just a function of the fact that every single helping professional, no matter how well educated and experienced, is also a human being. And human beings are subject to vulnerabilities, including lapses in knowledge and mistakes in judgment.

Nonetheless, I am a big believer in the value of learning from mistakes. In fact, during my longer training programs where therapist participants have opportunities to apply many of the principles and techniques they are learning, I heartily encourage them to make mistakes. When assigning a practice session I routinely declare, "Whoever makes the most mistakes will learn the most." And I mean it. A professional training program is a marvelous place to make and learn from mistakes, particularly when practicing with colleagues who are role-playing clients rather than working on their own fragile issues (as I assign during these courses). Of course it is less desirable to make mistakes with actual clients, but it is unavoidable. It is also *rare* that therapeutic errors are irretrievable or irreparable.

Over the years, learning from many (if not most) of my own mistakes and those of my colleagues, supervisees, and trainees, I have gathered a collection of (what I believe are) common trauma treatment blunders. I am sharing them here accompanied by a final disclaimer, with the aim that my and their errors will help you to avoid some of the most usual ones yourself.

What I am calling an *error* or *mistake* in this section is completely a result of my own opinion based on my observations of the difficulties that arose in a wide range of therapeutic situations and the variety of repairs that appeared to fix them.

Language Matters

How both therapist and client speak about traumatic incidents has an actual impact on how those incidents are perceived and felt. In Chapter 3, for instance, I discussed the importance of defining a flashback as a memory, which it is. That is an illustration of using precise language to clarify what is being dealt with. In this section, additional examples of ways in which specific word choices can be used to clarify and simplify issues and procedures pertinent to trauma treatment, both for recovery and memory resolution, will be discussed. An argument for paying closer attention to how therapists and their clients talk about past traumatic incidents, along with alternatives for more accurate formulations, will be proposed.

Verb Tense

As you already know, probably all too well, dealing with traumatic stress can be very tricky. The hallmark phenomenon of flashback, when intense memory of the distressing incident causes it to feel as if it is happening (again or still) in the present, makes trauma treatment completely differ-ent, and much more volatile than most other types of psychotherapy and counseling. When traumatic memories are provoked, it can be very con-fusing for the client, and also sometimes the therapist, to know not only *what* is happening but also *when* it is happening. It is common for clients as well as their therapists to talk about trauma with present-tense verbs: "I *am* walking down the street," "He *is* following me," in pursuing Phase 2 resolution of trauma memories. When a client is having a flashback or processing a memory, there is also widespread use of questions such as, "Where are you?" (meaning where the trauma happened), or "How old are you?" (meaning the age of the client back then).

No matter when a traumatic incident happened, unless it is actually occurring in your office in the moment you are talking with your client (and hopefully it is not), the incident happened in the past. That is true if it was 40 years ago, last week, or even yesterday. In psychotherapy and body psychotherapy, long before trauma therapy became a specialty, it was common when remembering and working through the distress of a past event to speak of it as if it was happening now, using present-tense verbs. It was not a particularly good idea then. And now, as we become more wise, adept, and focused on helping people with their traumatic memories—either to contain them (recovery, Phase 1) or to work through them (resolution, Phase 2) precise verb tense usage will greatly facilitate that process.

Think about it—it's actually common sense as well as the truth that the trauma happened in the past. So sticking to past-tense verbs when referring to it only promotes that truth. Recognizing that separating past from present is a major task of both trauma recovery and trauma memory resolution, it really makes sense to talk and think about it as is true: it is in the past. *Was*, not is. *Happened*, not happening. *Were*, not are. And so on.

Reliving vs. Remembering

The vocabulary of the trauma professionals, also authors, often includes the labeling of flashbacks as "reliving" or "reexperiencing" a traumatic event. To be honest, both of those terms confuse me as I cannot see how something that happened in the past can be lived or experienced *again*. While I and most in the trauma field would agree that the *nervous system* of an individual with PTSD continues to *react as if* the traumatic incident was happening again or still, vocabulary that implies that is the case does not help the individual to distinguish past from present. The truth is that a traumatic incident from the past can*not* be "relived." There is no time machine that would make it possible. Even when the current experience of past trauma is intense (and it is usually very, very intense), that is not reliving or even reexperiencing. Simply, it is *remembering*. All of those intense experiences of past trauma, whether recalled in visual or auditory images, bodily sensations, or reenacting behaviors, are all forms of remembering that experience.

While I do not have statistics, I can tell you that I and many of my supervisees and trainees have found that eliminating reliving and reexperiencing from our vocabularies and repeatedly reminding clients that their flashbacks are memories have a stabilizing and sane-making impact.

Memories of Resources vs. Memories of Trauma

Following from the section above, it is important to also discuss how to reference and use the memory of resources (as highlighted in Chapter 6), including what some call *anchors* or *safe places*. Often a therapist (including myself in times past) will encourage clients to imagine a resource, say their dog, favorite teacher, or grandfather, is *in the therapy room* alongside them. Many clients take well to this type of imaginary support; however, there is an inherent risk in this practice that I would like to point out.

As mentioned before, working with PTSD means constantly and persistently fighting against a belief or impression that the traumatic event is happening still or again. Much of trauma treatment involves helping clients to distinguish highly distressing memories from the actual present moment where safety is (usually) to be had. Such distinction is integral to both Phase 1 trauma recovery and Phase 2 trauma memory resolution.

If it is important to recognize intrusions of past trauma as a kind of memory, it must be the same when accessing *good* memories (resources, anchors, safe places). Images from the past, whether pleasant or unpleasant, are *all* memories. Consistency in this regard will reduce potential confusions such as, "You're trying to convince me that the man who molested me when I was 6 years old is *not* here in this room at the same time that you want me to imagine my favorite childhood dog *is*?"

Assumptions and Timing

In the second chapter I wrote about the particular importance of precision in working with traumatized individuals. ANS observation is a relatively objective way to increase the care of the treatment you provide. Below, I will discuss additional areas where greater attention, along with liberal applications of common sense, might also help to ease some of the inherent difficulties of trauma treatment.

Intuition vs. Knowledge

While I and nearly all psychotherapists rely somewhat on intuition, doing so exclusively is not advised when dealing with trauma. And that can be a challenge for those therapists who have learned, been trained, or decided to depend fully (or at least in large part) on their intuition. While in many areas of psychotherapy working in the context of intuition can be very useful, in dealing with clients with PTSD it can be hazardous.

In several popular dictionaries (*Webster's*, Google Online, Oxford Online), the definition of intuition is virtually alike. They all basically agree that intuition is a type of knowledge that is acquired *without* reason. And therein lie the limitations of relying on intuition when dealing with traumatized clients. The highly sensitive and volatile dysregulated nervous system of individuals with PTSD is much too easily disrupted to risk making interventions that you have not checked against reason, theory, principles, and common sense. Working with PTSD is not the kind of therapeutic milieu where following the client's process or the therapist's hunch is a good idea. The risks are just too great for disaster to ensue.

On the other hand, this does not mean that you should throw out your intuition when working with PTSD. It is too valuable to be ignored. However, it will be safer and even more useful if you first check it against your knowledge: of the client, of the current goal (what are we making?), how a hunch or feeling jives with known theory, and so on. To do that may sometimes require taking a pause rather than impulsively charging ahead. First take a few seconds or a minute to think, to consider. Clients will never mind your taking a think break so long as they know you are thinking about them and not what you need to buy or ruminating on a personal problem. If your hit of intuition jives with your knowledge of principles and theory, proceed on. However, if your intuition is at odds with what you know, you might need to lay it aside.

Intuition can also increase in value, and safety, when checked with the client before assuming it is correct or the right way to go. You might ask, for example, "This is what I am thinking (or is my hunch). Does that have meaning for you? . . . or seem like a good idea?" or some such.

Curiosity

Managing curiosity can be difficult for many trauma therapists. Curiosity, like so many human traits, has advantages as well as disadvantages. It is a major ally that brings many practitioners to this work to begin with. Psychotherapists are curious about how humans function and what shapes them into the personalities they become. To one degree or another as a profession, we (me included) are human behavior voyeurs. Therapists are interested to know about their clients; that is why they do what they do. Curiosity also helps to drive enthusiasm for their work, energizing therapists to be interested and listen intently.

However, curiosity unchecked can hinder a process, or even put a client into a danger zone. Really? Really! Think about the first interview with a new trauma client. The therapist needs to get to know the client's history, including a listing of the traumas she has experienced and the ones she wants to work on. But stopping with just basic information such as, "There was a rape," "I lost my husband in a tsunami," "the war was awful," can be difficult to contain. In Chapter 3 managing the client's insistence to tell his story was addressed, but the therapist's curiosity can also play a role. It is easy, sometimes a habit, to allow the client go on with her trauma story, especially when the therapist wants to know what happened, wants to know the details. However, how much does the therapist need to know in that first session to be able to move forward with the client? Does the therapist really need the details about, for example, *how* a rape occurred, or is the fact that it happened enough, at least initially? It is also worth considering if *all* details actually need to be narrated in the Phase 2 processing of trauma memories. Of course, bearing witness can be therapeutic, but does the narrative need to include every element? I do not have a conclusive answer, but I consider it a question worth pondering. This is an area where I believe the traditions of trauma treatment may have gone awry. While I do agree that telling the fact of a trauma is helpful and that disclosing physical or sexual abuse is necessary, I am not convinced that going over all of the details is indicated in either of those situations. There is also another concern: Many trauma therapists suffer consequences of curiosity themselves. Vicarious traumatization is a legitimate risk factor for therapists and often results from listening to and empathizing with highly detailed client stories.

All in all, I believe it is important for every trauma therapist to, at least at times, be able to contain his curiosity. Sometimes it may be better for the client, and sometimes it may be better for the therapist, simply to not know.

Timing

Those who are paying for the skills and expertise of the trauma therapist are all in a hurry: the insurance companies, the directors and boards of clinics and nonprofits, employers, and, not least of all, clients. It is understandable, but for the most part it is not helpful. One of my favorite quotes from Lewis Carroll, mentioned also in Chapter 7, "The hurrier I go, the behinder I get," is also apt for trauma treatment that is pushed by employer and insurance demands. This can result in regression, that is, a client's condition worsening. Chapter 1 was devoted to a discussion of the advantages of spending adequate time in Phase 1 treatment, securing stabilization and safety before heading into Phase 2 trauma memory processing. So I find it unfortunate when therapists and traumatized clients are restricted to (typically) 6 to 10 sessions with the expectation that the trauma memory will be resolved in that time. Frequently, in supervision, consultation, and professional trainings, I get asked what to do in such circumstances. The only commonsense solution I can think of (short of obtaining an adequate amount of sessions) is to stick to Phase 1 following the adage to "first do no harm."

Acknowledgments

I could not have written this book without the wonderful support of family, close friends, and colleagues, literally around the world. Each of them warmed my heart, sustained my spirit, and stimulated my thinking. . . . Thank you, *thank you*!

- *United Kingdom*: Michael Gavin, Kathrin Stauffer, Gillian Chumbley
- *Ireland*: Patricia Bourke D'Souza, Gillford D'Souza
- *Australia*: Peter King, Sarah McGregor
- *USA*: Rachelle Elias, Dora Lendvai Wischik, Linda Curran, David Grill, Christiane Wolf, Janina Fisher, Teddy Tapscott
- *Denmark*: Merete Holm Brantbjerg, Marianne Williams Bentzen

Additional thanks are specially extended to Patricia Bourke D'Souza for making the fold-out color ANS table beautiful and perfect, and to Merete Holm Brantbjerg for generously sharing her extensive knowledge of low-energy states.

Were it possible to love one's publishing house, I would say, without a doubt, *I love W. W. Norton!* Everyone there has always believed in, supported, and been patient with me through easy and difficult times. Deborah Malmud has been my loyal editor (I nearly wrote "therapist") for most of that time. Thank you, Deborah, for your support and humor, and for always being incredibly *encourageable*. In addition, I want to thank Kevin Olsen for his marketing acumen, Elisabeth Kerr for seeing my books translated into over a dozen languages, and Elizabeth Baird for attending to every detail. Grateful thanks to you all!

References

Alim, T. N., Feder, A., Graves, R. E., Wang, Y., Weaver, J., Westphal, M., Alonso, A., Aigbogun, N. U., Smith, B. W., Doucette, J. T., Mellman, T. A., Lawson, W. B., & Charney, D. S. (2008). Trauma, resilience, and recovery in a high-risk African-American population. *American Journal of Psychiatry, 165*(12), 1566–1575.

American Psychiatric Association. (1968). *Diagnostic and statistical manual of mental disorders* (2nd ed.). Washington, DC: Author.

American Psychiatric Association. (2013). Diagnostic and statistical manual of mental disorders (5th ed.). Washington, DC: Author.

Angelou, M. (1969). *I know why the caged bird sings.* New York: Random House.

Baraz, J., & Lilyana, M. (2016). *Awakening joy for kids.* Berkeley: Parallax.

Baumker, W. H. (1978). The magic shop. In C. Moiso (Ed.), *Transactional analysis in Europe: Contributions to EATA conferences, 1977–1978* (pp. 130–135). Rome: EATA.

Berne, E. (1964). *Games people play: The basic handbook of transactional analysis.* New York: Ballantine.

Bisson, I., Ehlers, A., Mathews, R., Pilling, S., Richards, D., & Turner, S. (2007). Psychological treatments for chronic post-traumatic stress disorder: Systematic review and meta-analysis. *British Journal of Psychiatry, 190*(2), 97–104.

Boon, S., Steele, K., & van der Hart, O. (2001). *Coping with trauma related dissociation.* New York: Norton.

Booth, R. (2014, August 24). Mindfulness therapy comes at a high price for some, say experts. *Guardian.* Retrieved from https://www.theguardian.com/society/2014/aug/25/mental-health-meditation

Brantbjerg, M. H. (2012). Hyporesponse: The hidden challenge in coping with stress. *International Body Psychotherapy Journal, 11*(2), 95–118. Retrieved from: http://www.ibpj.org/issues/articles/Holm%20Brantbjerg%20-%20Hyporesponse.pdf

Burnap, G. W. (1848). *The sphere and duties of woman: A course of lectures.* London: John Murphy.

Child Sexual Abuse Task Force and Research and Practice Core, National Child Traumatic Stress Network. (2004). *How to implement trauma-focused cognitive behavioral therapy.* Durham, NC: National Center for Child Traumatic Stress.

Chu, J. A. (2011). *The therapeutic roller coaster: Phase-oriented treatment for com-*

plex ptsd in rebuilding shattered lives: Treating complex ptsd and dissociative disorders (2nd ed.). Hoboken, NJ: John Wiley.

Cloitre, M., Courtois, C. A., Ford, J. D., Green, B. L., Alexander, P., Briere, J., Herman, J. L., Lanius, R., Stolbach, B. C., Spinazzola, J., van der Kolk, B. A., & van der Hart, O. (2012). The ISTSS expert consensus treatment guidelines for complex PTSD in adults. Retrieved from http://www.traumacenter.org/products/pdf_files/ISTSS_Complex_Trauma_Treatment_Guidelines_2012_Cloitre,Courtois,Ford,Green,Alexander,Briere,Herman,Lanius,Stolbach,Spinazzola,van%20der%20Kolk,van%20der%20Hart.pdf

Courtois, C. (1999). *Recollections of sexual abuse: Treatment principles and guidelines.* New York: Norton.

Courtois, C. A., & Ford, J. D. (2013). *Treating complex trauma: A sequenced, relationship-based approach.* New York: Guilford.

Curran, L. A. (2010). *Trauma competency: A clinician's guide.* Eau Claire, WI: PESI.

Curran, L. (Director/Producer). (2012). *Trauma treatment: Psychotherapy for the 21st century.* Eau Claire, WI: Premier Publishing and Media.

Damasio, A. (1994). Descartes' error. New York: Avon.

Defense Centers of Excellence. (2013). *Posttraumatic stress disorder pocket guide: To accompany the 2010 VA/DoD clinical practice guideline for the management of posttraumatic stress.* Washington, DC: Department of Veterans Affairs. Retrieved from http://www.healthquality.va.gov/guidelines/MH/ptsd/PTSDPocketGuide23May2013v1.pdf

Fallot, R. D., & Harris, M. (2001). A trauma-informed approach to screening and assessment. *New Directions for Mental Health Services, 89,* 23–31.

Feldenkrais, M. (1972). *Awareness through movement: Health exercises for personal growth.* New York: Harper and Row.

Felitti, V. J., Anda, R. F., Nordenberg, D., Williamson, D. F., Spitz, A. M., Edwards, V., Koss, M. P., & Marks, J. S. (1998). Relationship of childhood abuse and household dysfunction to many of the leading causes of death in adults. *American Journal of Preventive Medicine, 14*(4), 245–258.

Fisher, J. (1999). The work of stabilization in trauma treatment. Paper presented at the Trauma Center Lecture Series 1999, Boston. Retrieved from http://www.janinafisher.com/pdfs/stabilize.pdf

Fisher, J. (2009). Self-harm and suicidality. *Interact: Journal of the Trauma and Abuse Group UK, 9,* 2.

Forbes, D., Creamer, M., Bisson, J. I., Cohen, J. A., Crow, B. E., Foa, E. B., Friedman, M. J., Keane, T. M., Kudler, H. S., & Ursano, R. J. (2010). A guide to guidelines for the treatment of PTSD and related conditions. *Journal of Traumatic Stress, 23*(5), 537–552.

Ford, J. D., Courtois, C. A., Steele, K., Van der Hart, O., & Nijenhuis, E. R. S. (2005). Treatment of complex posttraumatic self-dysregulation. *Journal of Traumatic Stress, 18*, 437–447. doi:10.1002/jts.20051

Gallup, G. 1977. Tonic immobility: Evolutionary underpinnings of human catalepsy and catatonia. In M. E. P. Seligman & J. D. Maser (Eds.), *Pathopathology: Experimental models* (pp. 334–357). San Francisco: W. H. Freeman.

Garden, M. (2007, September/October). Can meditation be bad for you? *The Humanist.*

Gerger, H., Munder, T., Gemperli, A., Nüesch, E., Trelle, S., Jüni, P., & Barth, J. (2014). Integrating fragmented evidence by network meta-analysis: Relative effectiveness of psychological interventions for adults with post-traumatic stress disorder. *Psychological Medicine, 44*, 3151–3164.

Harris, M., & Fallot, R. D. (2001). Envisioning a trauma-informed service system: A vital paradigm shift. *New Directions for Mental Health Services, 89*(Spring).

Harrison, R. L. (2007). *Preventing vicarious traumatization of mental health therapists: Identifying protective practices* (Unpublished doctoral thesis). University of British Columbia, BC, Canada.

Heide, F. J., & Borkovec, T. D. (1983). Relaxation-induced anxiety: Paradoxical anxiety enhancement due to relaxation training. *Journal of Consulting and Clinical Psychology, 51*(2), 171–182.

Herman, J. (1992). *Trauma and recovery.* New York: Basic Books.

Howorth, P. (2000). The treatment of shellshock: Cognitive therapy before its time. *Psychiatric Bulletin, 24*, 225–227.

Huff, D. (1954). *How to lie with statistics.* New York: Norton.

Imel, Z. E., Laska, K., Jakupcak, M., & Simpson, T. L. (2013). Meta-analysis of dropout in treatments for posttraumatic stress disorder. *Journal of Consulting and Clinical Psychology, 81*(3), 394–404.

Ioannidis, J. P. A. (2005). Why most published research findings are false. *PLoS Medicine, 2*(8), e124. Retrieved from http://robotics.cs.tamu.edu/RSS2015NegativeResults/pmed.0020124.pdf

Janet, P. (1886). Les actes inconscientes et la memoire pendant le somnambulisme. *Revue Philosophique, 25*(1), 238–279.

Janet, P. (1898). Le traitement psychologique de l'hysterie. In A. Robin (Ed.), *Traite de therapeutique appliquee.* Paris: Rueff.

Janet, P. (1976). *Les medications psychologiques* (Vol. 3).New York: Arno. (Original work published 1919, Paris: Felix Alcan)

Kabat-Zinn, J. (1990). *Full catastrophe living: Using the wisdom of your body and mind to face stress, pain, and illness.* New York: Deltacorte.

Lang, C. (2016, July/August). Narrative therapy approaches in the treatment of trauma. *The Therapist*, 14–17.

Langley, J. N. (1903). The autonomic nervous system. *Brain, 26*, 1–26.

Le, Q. A., Doctor, J. N., Zoellner, L. A., & Feeny, N. C. (2014). Cost-effectiveness of prolonged exposure therapy versus pharmacotherapy and treatment choice in posttraumatic stress disorder (the Optimizing PTSD Treatment Trial): A doubly randomized preference trial. *Journal of Clinical Psychiatry, 75*(3), 222–230.

Lee, K. A., Villant, G. E., Torrey, W. C., & Elder, G. H. (1995). A 50-year prospective study of the psychological sequelae of World War II combat. *American Journal of Psychiatry, 152*(4), 516–522.

Lehrer, P. M., & Woolfolk, R. L. (1993). Specific effects of stress management techniques. In P. M. Lehrer & R. L. Woolfolk (Eds.), *Principles and practice of stress management*. New York: Guilford.

Levine, P. (1992). *The body as healer: Transforming trauma and anxiety.* Lyons, CO: Author.

Levine, P. (1997). *Waking the tiger: Healing trauma.* Berkeley: North Atlantic.

Levine, P. (2010). *In an unspoken voice.* Berkeley: North Atlantic.

Linehan, M. (1993). *Cognitive-behavioral treatment of borderline personality disorder.* New York: Guilford.

Linehan, M. (2014). *DBT Skills Training Manual* (2nd rev. ed.). New York: Guilford.

Management of Post-Traumatic Stress Working Group. (2010). *VA/DoD clinical practice guideline for the management of post-traumatic stress.* Washington, DC: Department of Veterans Affairs. Retrieved from http://www.healthquality.va.gov/guidelines/MH/ptsd/cpgPTSDFULL201011612c.pdf

MedlinePlus. 2015. Shock. In *Medical encyclopedia*. Retrieved from http://www.nlm.nih.gov/medlineplus/ency/article/000039.htm

Mental Health Daily. (2015). Relaxation-induced anxiety: Potential causes and solutions. Retrieved from http://mentalhealthdaily.com/2015/03/15/relaxation-induced-anxiety-potential-causes-solutions/

Mullen, M.-F. (2012, May 26). Some rules for teaching yoga to students with PTSD. *Elephant Journal*. Retrieved from http://www.elephantjournal.com/2012/05/some-rules-for-teaching-yoga-to-students-with-ptsd-mark-francis-mullen/

National Center for PTSD. (2013). *Understanding PTSD treatment.* Washington, DC: U.S. Department of Veterans Affairs.

National Institute for Health Care Excellence. (2005). *Post-traumatic stress disorder (PTSD): The management of PTSD in adults and children in primary and secondary care.* London: Author. Retrieved from http://www.coe.int/t/dg4/majorhazards/ressources/virtual library/materials/uk/CG026NICEguideline.pdf

Ogden, P., Minton, K., & Pain, C. (2006). *Trauma and the body.* New York: Norton.

Perls, F. (1942). *Ego, hunger and aggression: The beginning of Gestalt therapy.* New York: Random House.

Perls, F. (1968). *Gestalt therapy verbatim.* Moab, U   T: Real People.

Petzold, H. (1971). Die therapeutischen Möglichkeiten der psychodramatischen "Magic Shop"-Technik. *Zeitschrift für klinische Psychologie und Psychotherapie, 19*(4), 354–369.

Porges, S. (2001). The polyvagal theory: Phylogenetic substrates of a social nervous system. *International Journal of Psychophysiology, 42,* 123–146.

Porges, S. (2011). *The polyvagal theory: Neurophysiologial foundations of emotions, attachment, communication, and self-regulation.* New York: Norton.

Rankin, A. C. (1978, May/June). Standards for yoga teachers. *Yoga Journal, 20,* 45–47.

Rivers, W. H. R. (1918). An address on the repression of war experience. *Lancet,* 191(4927), 173–177.

Ronconi, J. M., Shiner, B., & Watts, B. V. (2014). Inclusion and exclusion criteria in randomized controlled trials of psychotherapy for PTSD. *Journal of Psychiatric Practice, 20*(1), 25–37.

Rothschild, B. (1993). A shock primer for the body-psychotherapist. *Energy and Character, 24,* 1.

Rothschild, B. (2000). *The body remembers: The psychophysiology of trauma and trauma treatment.* New York: Norton.

Rothschild, B. (2003). *The body remembers casebook: Unifying methods and models in the treatment of trauma and PTSD.* New York: Norton.

Rothschild, B. (2004, January–February). Applying the brakes. *Psychotherapy Networker.*

Rothschild, B. (2006). *Help for the helper: The psychophysiology of compassion fatigue and vicarious trauma.* New York: Norton.

Rothschild, B. (2010). *8 keys to safe trauma recovery: Take-charge strategies to empower your healing.* New York: Norton.

Rothschild, B. (2011). *Trauma essentials: The go-to guide.* New York: Norton.

Schutzenberger, A. A. (1965). *Precis de psychodrama.* Paris: Editions Universitaires.

Siegel, D. J. (1999). *The developing mind.* New York: Guilford.

Siegel, D. J. (2010). *Mindsight: The new science of personal transformation.* New York: Bantam.

Spinazzola, J., Blaustein, M., & van der Kol k, B. A. (2005). Posttraumatic stress disorder treatment outcome research: The study of unrepresentative samples. *Journal of Traumatic Stress, 18*(5), 425–436.

Thompson, I. A., Amatea, E. S., & Thompson, E. S. (2014). Personal and contextual predictors of mental health counselors' compassion fatigue and burnout. *Journal of Mental Health Counseling,*36(1), 58–77.

Treleaven, D. (in press). *Trauma-Sensitive Mindfulness: Practices for Safe Healing.* New York: Norton.

van der Hart, O. (2012). The use of imagery in phase 1 treatment of clients with complex dissociative disorders. *European Journal of Psychotraumatology, 3.* http://dx.doi.org/10.3402/ejpt.v3i0.8458

van der Hart, O., Brown, P., & van der Kolk, B. A. (1989). Pierre Janet's treatment of post-traumatic stress. *Journal of Traumatic Stress, 2*(4), 379–395.

van der Hart, O., Nijenhuis, E. R. S., & Steele, K. (2006). *The haunted self.* New York: Norton.

van der Kolk, B. A. (2001). EMDR, consciousness and the body. In F. Shapiro (Ed.), *EMDR: Promises for a paradigm shift.* Washington, DC: American Psychological Press.

Wampold, B. E., Imel, Z. E., Laska, K. M., Benish, S., Miller, S. D., Flückiger, C., Del Re, A. C., Baardseth, T. P., & Budge, S. (2010). Determining what works in the treatment of PTSD. *Clinical Psychology Review, 30,* 923–933.

Watters, E. (2010). *Crazy like us: The globalization of the American psyche.* New York: Free Press.

Watts, B. V., Schnurr, P. P., Mayo, L., Young-Xu, Y., Weeks, W. B., & Friedman, M. J. (2013). Meta-analysis of the efficacy of treatments for posttraumatic stress disorder. *Journal of Clinical Psychiatry, 74*(6), 541–550.

Wylie, M. S. (2015, January/February). The mindfulness explosion. *Psychotherapy Networker.*

Index